# Classroom Assessment and the
## *National Science Education Standards*

Committee on Classroom Assessment and
the *National Science Education Standards*

J. Myron Atkin, Paul Black, Janet Coffey,
*Editors*

Center for Education

Division of Behavioral and Social Sciences
and Education

National Research Council

## National Academy Press
Washington, D.C.

**NATIONAL ACADEMY PRESS • 2101 Constitution Avenue, NW • Washington, DC 20418**

NOTICE: The project that is the subject of this report was approved by the Governing Board of the National Research Council, whose members are drawn from the councils of the National Academy of Sciences, the National Academy of Engineering, and the Institute of Medicine. The members of the committee responsible for the report were chosen for their special competences and with regard for appropriate balance.

This study was supported by Contract/Grant No. ES1 9618770 and NCC5-247 between the National Academy of Sciences, National Science Foundation, and NASA, respectively. Any opinions, findings, conclusions, or recommendations expressed in this publication are those of the author(s) and do not necessarily reflect the views of the organizations or agencies that provided support for the project.

**Library of Congress Cataloging-in-Publication Data**

Classroom assessment and the National Science Education Standards / Committee on Classroom Assessment and the National Science Education Standards ; J. Myron Atkin, Paul Black, Janet Coffey, editors.
    p. cm.
    Includes bibliographical references and index.
    ISBN 0-309-06998-X (pbk.)
    1. Science—Ability testing—United States.  2. Science—Study and teaching—United States—Evaluation.  3. Science—Study and teaching—Standards—United States.    I. Atkin, J. Myron. II. Black, Paul. III. Coffey, Janet. IV. National Research Council (U.S.). Committee on Classroom Assessment and the National Science Education Standards.
    LB1585.3 .C54 2001
    371.27—dc21

                      2001001252

Suggested citation: National Research Council. (2001). *Classroom assessment and the National Science Education Standards.* Committee on Classroom Assessment and the *National Science Education Standards.* J. Myron Atkin, Paul Black, and Janet Coffey (Eds.). Center for Education, Division of Behavioral and Social Sciences and Education. Washington, DC: National Academy Press.

Additional copies of this report are available from National Academy Press, 2101 Constitution Avenue, N.W., Lockbox 285, Washington, D.C. 20055; (800) 624-6242 or (202) 334-3313 (in the Washington metropolitan area); Internet, http://www.nap.edu

Printed in the United States of America

# THE NATIONAL ACADEMIES

National Academy of Sciences
National Academy of Engineering
Institute of Medicine
National Research Council

The **National Academy of Sciences** is a private, nonprofit, self-perpetuating society of distinguished scholars engaged in scientific and engineering research, dedicated to the further-ance of science and technology and to their use for the general welfare. Upon the authority of the charter granted to it by the Congress in 1863, the Academy has a mandate that requires it to advise the federal government on scientific and technical matters. Dr. Bruce M. Alberts is president of the National Academy of Sciences.

The **National Academy of Engineering** was established in 1964, under the charter of the National Academy of Sciences, as a parallel organization of outstanding engineers. It is autonomous in its administration and in the selection of its members, sharing with the National Academy of Sciences the responsibility for advising the federal government. The National Academy of Engineering also sponsors engineering programs aimed at meeting national needs, encourages education and research, and recognizes the superior achievements of engineers. Dr. William A. Wulf is president of the National Academy of Engineering.

The **Institute of Medicine** was established in 1970 by the National Academy of Sciences to secure the services of eminent members of appropriate professions in the examination of policy matters pertaining to the health of the public. The Institute acts under the responsibility given to the National Academy of Sciences by its congressional charter to be an adviser to the federal government and, upon its own initiative, to identify issues of medical care, research, and education. Dr. Kenneth I. Shine is president of the Institute of Medicine.

The **National Research Council** was organized by the National Academy of Sciences in 1916 to associate the broad community of science and technology with the Academy's purposes of furthering knowledge and advising the federal government. Functioning in accordance with general policies determined by the Academy, the Council has become the principal operating agency of both the National Academy of Sciences and the National Academy of Engineering in providing services to the government, the public, and the scientific and engineering communi-ties. The Council is administered jointly by both Academies and the Institute of Medicine. Dr. Bruce M. Alberts and Dr. William A. Wulf are chairman and vice chairman, respectively, of the National Research Council.

# Preface

The Committee on Science Education K-12 (COSE K-12) is a group of volunteer advisors within the National Research Council's (NRC) Center for Education (CFE). Since the publication of the *National Science Education Standards* (the *Standards*) in 1996, an important part of the mission of COSE K-12 has been to monitor and analyze the application and impact of the *Standards* on the practices, programs, and policies of American science education. The *Standards* were developed over the course of four years, involving tens of thousands of educators and scientists in extensive comment and review. The resultant standards offered advice to be applied voluntarily by educators and policymakers persuaded by the vision of effective science education for all students and by the credibility of the authors and the processes used to reach consensus. It became apparent to the members of COSE K-12 that the necessarily broad, visionary nature of the *Standards* did not provide suffi-

cient guidance or develop a sufficiently deep understanding of key topics needed for implementation.

The highest priority topics requiring more detail and guidance were identified as:

- scientific inquiry as content as well as an approach to teaching science,
- assessment by teachers and the students to improve learning,
- the place for technology in the science curriculum,
- selection and identification of effective instructional materials aligned with standards, and
- development of a coherent science program for 13 years of schooling.

For each topic, a group of experts was convened with an appropriate balance of viewpoint, experience, and expertise in the research base. Each group was charged to develop a publication that developed a deeper understanding of the topic, compiled and analyzed research and resources, and provided guidance for implementation through programs and policies at the local level.

This volume addresses the second point and joins a series published within the last two years including: *Inquiry and the National Science Education Standards* (NRC, 2000), *Selecting Instructional Materials: A Guide for K-12 Science* (NRC, 1999), and *Designing Mathematics or Science Curriculum Programs: A Guide for Using Mathematics and Science Education Standards* (NRC, 1999). COSE K-12 also developed a guide for parents and other community members entitled *Every Child a Scientist: Achieving Scientific Literacy for All* (NRC, 1998), which was concerned with the improvement of science education and addressed common questions, as well as promoted informed local action. These and all publications of the National Academy Press are available on the Internet at http://www.nap.edu.

The committee would like to thank several people for the significant help they provided in the preparation of this report. At the project's conception, Rodger Bybee was Executive Director of the Center for Science, Mathematics, and Engineering Education (CSMEE) at the National Research Council. Susan Loucks-Horsley was program officer for COSE K-12. Both were enthusiastic about the project and swiftly identified and allocated the resources that would make the report a reality. Susan died tragically before the project's completion. We would like to believe that she would be pleased by this report's emphasis on the centrality of teacher professional development in improving assessment in the classroom.

Jane Butler Kahle, Chair of COSE K-12 when the project was approved, was instrumental in choosing the focus on assessment in the classroom as a priority for the committee. Kathy Comfort, Carolyn Ray, and Rachel Wood were active participants in the deliberations about the main emphasis of the document and its organization. All three provided many of the examples that appear throughout the document. On behalf of the NRC, Jan Tuomi assumed the administrative reins for COSE K-12 about half way through the project. She expertly helped to bring it to a conclusion, and, in particular, shepherded the manuscript skillfully through the complex and exacting NRC review procedure. Others who made significant contributions included Doug Sprunger, the COSE K-12 senior administrative associate, and Kirsten Sampson Snyder, CFE Reports Officer.

This report has been reviewed in draft form by individuals chosen for their diverse perspectives and technical expertise, in accordance with procedures approved by the NRC's Report Review Committee. The purpose of this independent review is to provide candid and critical comments that will assist the institution in making its published report as sound as possible and to ensure that the report meets institutional standards for objectivity, evidence, and responsiveness to the study charge. The review comments and draft manuscript remain confidential to protect the integrity of the deliberative process. We wish to thank the following individuals for their review of this report: **Jerry A. Bell**, American Chemical Society, Washington, DC; **Lloyd Bond**, University of North Carolina, Greensboro; **Lucy Eubanks**, Clemson University; **Senta Raizen,** National Center for Improving Science Education, Washington, DC; **Lorrie A. Shepard**, University of Colorado, Boulder; **Stephen G. Sireci**, University of Massachusetts, Amherst; **Richard Stiggins**, Assessment Training Institute, Portland, OR; **Steven Weinberg**, Connecticut State Department of Education; and **Grant Wiggins**, Learning by Design, Pennington, NJ.

Although the reviewers listed above have provided many constructive comments and suggestions, they were not asked to endorse the conclusions or recommendations nor did they see the final draft of the report before its release. The review of this report was overseen by **Barbara Means** of SRI International, Menlo Park, CA. She was responsible for making certain that an independent examination of this report was carried out in accordance with institutional procedures and that all review comments were carefully considered. Responsibility for the final content of this report rests entirely with the authoring committee and the institution.

Sincerely,

J. Myron Atkin
Chair

# Contents

# Classroom
# Assessment and the
## *National Science Education Standards*

# Executive Summary

Assessment is a ubiquitous part of classroom life. Most exchanges between teacher and students are an occasion for considering the quality of student work. Often informal, assessment is a natural feature of teaching and learning whether or not it is so identified by teachers or students. A careful look at any classroom offers evidence of the intimate connection between teaching and assessment. It is at times difficult to separate the two.

In addition to the appraisals that are integrated into almost every teaching situation, there are the more formal assessments that also are part of ongoing classroom life and that most people think of first when asked about assessment: written or oral weekly quizzes, end-of-semester examinations, portfolios, and comments and grades on homework assignments. All these types of classroom assessment, the relatively formal and the less formal, are seen around the world as teachers work with students and as students work with each other.

Highlights of the findings in this report include the following:

- Research shows that regular and high-quality assessment in the classroom can have a positive effect on student achievement.

- The information generated **must be used** to inform the teacher and/or the students in deciding the next step. The results provide effective assessment to improve learning and teaching.

- Student participation is a key component of successful assessment strategies at every step. If students are to participate effectively in the process, they need to **be clear about the target and the criteria** for good work, to **assess their own efforts** in light of the criteria, and to **share responsibility in taking action** in light of the feedback.

- Teachers need time and assistance in developing accurate and dependable assessments. Much of this assistance can be provided by creating settings in which teachers have opportunities to talk with one another about the quality of student work.

• The essential support for teachers (for example, time and opportunities to work with other teachers) can be created at the school level, but sometimes district and state-level resources are necessary.

• It is necessary to align assessment in the classroom with externally developed examinations, if the goals of science education are to be consistent and not confuse both teachers and students. At the very least, external examinations must not vitiate the goals of science education that are proffered in the *National Science Education Standards* (the *Standards*) (National Research Council [NRC], 1996).

Although this report focuses on classroom assessments, these are not the only types of assessment that occur in the lives of students in school. To many, they are not even the most important ones. Much of the public attention to assessment is linked to the large-scale, standardized examinations that are developed, and usually scored, outside the classroom. These include state- or district-mandated tests, Advanced Placement examinations, the Scholastic Achievement Test (SAT) and SAT II, the American College Testing Program (ACT), and less frequently, national and international tests, such as National Assess-ment of Educational Progress (NAEP) and Third International Mathematics and Science Study (TIMSS). These types of assessments occur much less frequently—often once a school year–and usually serve different purposes than the ongoing assessments made on a continuing basis by students and teachers.

Each of these assessments is important—those that occur in daily classroom interactions among teachers and students, those set by teachers at the end of a particular phase in the work, and those developed and administered by external agencies. Together, they serve multiple purposes: to help students learn, to illustrate and articulate the standards for quality work, to inform teaching, to guide curriculum selection, to monitor programs, to provide a basis for reporting concrete accomplishments to interested parties, for accountability, among others. No one assessment serves or can serve all the possible or desired aims of gauging students' knowledge and abilities, understanding the nature of their thinking, and supporting their learning.

This report was conceived as an addendum to the *Standards* (NRC, 1996). In December 1995, the *Standards* were released as the result of an effort that began in 1991. At that time, the President of the National Science Teachers Association (NSTA) and leaders from several other groups approached the Chairman of the

National Research Council (NRC) with the request that the NRC coordinate the development of national standards for science education. For the next four years, committees of teachers, scientists, administrators, and teacher educators worked together to produce drafts of the *Standards*, which were then released for extensive review and comment. The result was a document that offers a broad vision for science education, including standards for teaching, professional development, assessment, content, programs, and systems.

Although the *Standards* emphasize large-scale external testing and assessment as well as the types of assessment that occur regularly in the classroom, **this document takes a closer look at the ongoing assessment that occurs each day in classrooms between teachers and students**. The discussion encompasses a notion of assessment broader than testing; includes all of the activities for a student to reflect on and demonstrate their understandings, skills, and growth by describing the purposes they serve (and might serve); and illustrates how such assessments look in actual classrooms. There is research-based evidence that attention to this ongoing form of assessment, particularly formative assessment, is beneficial for student learning; and a framework for improving daily classroom assessment lays the foundation for what follows.

The relationships between the assessment that teachers and students do daily and the summative assessments that often drive curriculum, instruction, and assessment are examined and discussed. Examples are provided of how these classroom assessments can be integrated into a comprehensive system of assessment, including externally developed standardized tests, both to improve the quality of student work and to make sounder and more complete judgments about student accomplishments.

Finally, the document outlines some challenges to the entire educational system for teachers to be able to conduct the types of assessments in their own classrooms that result in students reaching the higher standards for learning and assessment proffered in the *Standards*.

## ORGANIZATION OF THE REPORT

In preparation of this document, the goals set forth by the Committee on Science Education (COSE K-12) were to:

• articulate a research-based rationale for helping teachers improve classroom assessment;
• clarify the concept of effective classroom assessment;
• provide illustrations and guides to development and selection of assessment processes and tools;
• assist teacher educators and staff

developers who will include assessment in their work with prospective and practicing teachers; and

• address issues that school and district decision makers face in their efforts to improve classroom assessment.

In response to this charge, this document is organized around six chapters:

■ Chapter 1, An Introduction to Assessment in the Science Classroom, broadly outlines the rationale for the content covered in the guide. This chapter also lays the groundwork for serious attention to the types of assessment teachers and their students perform daily and their direct effect on improving learning.

■ Chapter 2, The Case for Strengthening Assessment in the Science Classroom, provides a research base for the importance of understanding and improving the type of assessment in the classroom that improves learning and pays particular attention to the notion of formative assessment. Chapters 2 and 3 may be especially useful for classroom teachers as a guide for examining their practice.

■ Chapter 3, Assessment in the Classroom, takes a closer look at the roles and responsibilities of teachers and students in improving assessment and offers a guiding framework for thinking about formative assessment.

Chapters 3 and 5 relate directly to responsibilities of people in policy positions at school district, state, and national levels and, in particular, those who make decisions about the spectrum of assessment tools to be employed for accountability, for certifying student accomplishment, and for the improvement of teaching and learning.

■ Chapter 4, The Relationship between Formative and Summative Assessment—In the Classroom and Beyond, addresses the tensions inherent in the different purposes and roles that teachers play in assessment and offers suggestions for how these tensions can be mitigated. In addition to teachers and administrators, professional-development specialists and teacher educators may want to focus on this chapter.

■ Chapter 5, Professional Development, considers and illustrates the potential richness of the professional development of teachers when assessment is the cornerstone and suggests some features to consider when designing professional-development experiences.

■ Chapter 6, Beyond the Classroom—System-Level Supports, proposes how programs and systems can support teachers and students in improving the classroom assessments to develop learning. Parents and community members also may be interested in this discussion about the broader system level.

The document features a few vignettes of classroom activity wherein students and teachers are engaged in assessment. These vignettes are based on actual classroom experiences witnessed by committee members and other contributors to the report. The vignettes serve to illustrate key ideas in the text, not to represent idealized classroom scenarios.

We hope that *Classroom Assessment and the National Science Education Standards* will be used by a variety of people with responsibility for improving science education. Although we recommend reading the entire document, we acknowledge that particular chapters may speak to, or are more relevant for, particular audiences. Thus, throughout the document, sidebars indicate to the reader the particular audience for whom the material within a chapter or section may be particularly relevant. Within chapters, readers will find references to examples and points made in other chapters. We also believe parents will find these chapters of special interest.

# 1
# An Introduction to Assessment in the Science Classroom

This report elaborates on the *Standards* by providing a guide to optimize the ongoing activity in the science classroom that engages both teachers and students in making judgments about the students' quality of work and designing the necessary steps for improvement. This kind of assessment is universally present in schools and is a natural part of both teaching and learning. It is usually evidenced several times each hour as teachers and students ask questions, report on their assignments, and make decisions about what to do next. What are the goals? What differences exist between a student's current understanding and those goals? What can be done to close the gap? The primary aim of the assessment discussed here is to help students do higher quality work. The data collected and discussed in the process also can be used to convey important information about the students to parents and other interested adults.

This type of assessment, which is embedded in virtually every aspect of school life, is not the only kind that counts. The United States is in an era of large-scale testing, the like of which has not been seen since standardized tests were first introduced. During World War I, tests were administered to U.S. Army recruits that determined the specialties to which they would be assigned. In the 1920s, IQ tests were used extensively in the public education system to sort students into various school programs. Although they did not have the kind of life-or-death consequences associated with wartime assignments, they nevertheless counted heavily in determining a person's future. Those who scored well went into college-preparatory tracks; the others were assigned to less rigorous "general education" or to vocational programs. In the 1930s and 1940s, national examinations were introduced to provide data that figured in many college-admission decisions. However, all this testing of the past 85 years pales in comparison to the use of large-scale examinations today. At the beginning of the twenty-first century, new tests developed at the state or national level and administered to every student are used to rank public elementary and secondary schools, make decisions about their financial allocation from the state, decide if they will continue to be certified, and, in many places, directly determine teachers' salaries.

Depending on the grade level and the end use of the results, student examinations for these purposes, which usually take from 2 hours to 2 or 3 days, are used primarily for **selection** and **accountability**—selection of students for specialized instructional programs and account-ability to parents and other taxpayers regarding the effective use of public funds. Only indirectly are they administered to improve learning. When teachers and the public become aware of the test subject matter, classroom instruction begins to emphasize that content. Student scores rise as teachers teach to the test. Such examinations usually are given at the end of the school year, too late for the teacher to take remedial action with individual students. Often the teacher receives no information about the specific items that each student missed. Finally, the tests, which are typically designed to be machine-scored, do not cover the range of learning promoted in the *Standards*.

This document focuses on the importance and the **improvement** of the classroom-based element of a balanced system of assessment that includes both external tests and teachers' knowledge of the student's abilities. The *Standards* feature a range of objectives, including the ability of students to pursue a well-planned scientific investigation that may extend over several days, weeks, or even months. In this type of activity, the teacher makes judgments continually about the student's level of understanding by assisting the student during the course of the project and observing carefully the student's work, asking key questions along the way, and responding to the student's questions. The teacher continually probes the student to ensure how well the student understands the concept, to determine how they approach a problem, and to find out the assump-tions that underlie a student's re-sponse. During this process, the teacher has unique opportunities to make considered judgments, based on the concrete evidence collected about the quality of student accomplishment. With knowledge of the nature of a student's understanding, the teacher can act immediately on the basis of that information and does not have to rely solely on brief and often decontextualized responses or small samples of student work. A balanced and integrated system of assessment makes use of what the teacher knows.

Specifically, additional highlights of the document include the following:

- Research shows that regular and high-quality assessment in the classroom can have a positive effect on student achievement.
- The information generated **must be used** to inform the teacher and/or the students in deciding the next step. The results provide effective assessment to improve learning and teaching.
- Student participation is a key component of successful assessment strategies at every step. If students are to participate effectively in the process, they need to **be clear about the target and the criteria** for good work, to **assess their own efforts** in light of the criteria, and to **share responsibility in taking action** in light of the feedback.
- Teachers need time and assistance in developing accurate and dependable assessments. Much of this assistance can be provided by creating settings in which teachers have opportunities to talk with one another about the quality of student work.
- The essential support for teachers (for example, time and opportunities to work with other teachers) can be created at school level, but sometimes district and state-level resources are necessary.
- It is necessary to align assessment in the classroom with externally developed examinations if the goals of

science education are to be consistent and not confuse both teachers and students. At the very least, external examinations must not vitiate the goals of science education that are proffered in the *Standards*.

A major theme of this document is that improving the kind of assessment in the science classroom that leads to higher quality student work is not a matter solely of introducing new procedures, frameworks, techniques, rubrics, or guidelines. Because the kind of assessment described in this guide is so intricately rooted in how a teacher sees one's self (and is seen by the students), changing assessment practices in the ways suggested here is far from a mechanical act. A teacher, along with the students, becomes not only a judge of quality but also a designer of the plans necessary to meet the standards. For achievement to be raised, the teachers must help the **students themselves** learn how to make better judgments about the quality of their own work.

A contention in this document is that these kinds of changes in practice are intimately associated with how teachers view their own work as professionals. These changes will require fundamental reexamination of how teachers organize and conduct the class, as well as the kinds of relationships that are desired with students, school administrators, and parents. Redesigning classroom assessment in these suggested ways requires nothing less than the kind of deep reflection on the part of the teacher that frequently leads to a fundamental reorientation to what it means for teachers to teach and for students to learn.

# 2
# The Case for Strengthening Assessment in the Science Classroom

This chapter provides a rationale for this report: It presents a research base for the importance of understanding and improving the assessments that occur daily in classrooms that can directly influence learning. Teachers, teacher educators, administrators, and policy makers may find this chapter particularly relevant.

The goals for school science projected in the *Standards* represent a significant shift from traditional school practice. The document presents science as something that students actively do, rather than something that is done to or for them by teachers and texts. Science covers not only important facts but requires that objects and events be described carefully, that questions be asked about what is seen, that explanations of natural phenomena be constructed and tested, and that the resulting ideas be communicated to other people. It emphasizes the role of evidence in drawing conclusions. It involves making connections between students' current understandings of natural phenomena and the knowledge accepted and valued in the scientific community. Science also entails problem solving and decision making in the process of applying such knowledge to new situations and asking new questions. It is a way of knowing and thinking. If teachers can determine how well their students are meeting these new goals and students can learn how to gauge their progress, both can use this information to inform teaching and learning. By doing so, a vision for school science becomes a reality:

The *Standards* present a vision of a scientifically literate populace. They outline what students need to know, understand, and be able to do to be scientifically literate at different grade levels. They describe an educational system in which all students demonstrate high levels of performance, in which teachers are empowered to make the decisions essential for effective learning, in which interlocking communities of teachers and students are focused on learning science, and in which supportive educational programs and systems nurture achievement. (NRC, 1999, p. 2)

Expectations conveyed in the *Standards* call for assessment to meet the full range of goals for science education. To this end, a broad view of assessment is proffered, for example:

> Ideas about assessments have undergone important changes in recent years. In the new view, assessment and learning are two sides of the same coin… When students engage in assessments, they should learn from those assessments. (NRC, 1999, pp. 5-6)

Assessments that resonate with a standards-based reform agenda reflect the complexity of science as a discipline of interconnected ideas and as a way of thinking about the world. Assessments must not be only summative in nature, that is, offering a cumulative summary of achievement level, usually at the end of a unit or after a topic has been covered. These summative assessments can serve multiple purposes: they help to inform placement decisions and to communicate a judgment about performance to interested parties, including parents and students. Assessment also must become an integral and essential part of daily classroom activity.

Research supports the value that the standards document places on **formative** assessment in enriching students' understanding of science. Black and Wiliam (1998a) define formative assessment as, "all those activities undertaken by teachers and by their students [that] provide information to be used as feedback to modify the teaching and learning activities in which they are engaged" (p. 7). They conducted a major review of more than 250 articles and books (Black & Wiliam, 1998b) that present research evidence on assessment from several countries. The main conclusion as a result of their study was as follows:

> Standards are raised only by changes that are put into direct effect by teachers and students in classrooms. There is a body of firm evidence that formative assessment is an essential feature of classroom work and that development of it can raise standards. We know of no other way of raising standards for which such a strong *prima facie* case can be made on the basis of evidence of such large learning gains. (p. 19)

Assessment becomes formative in nature only when either the teacher or the student **uses** that information to inform teaching and/or to influence learning. Therefore, data from summative assessments can be used in formative ways. In practice, it may be difficult to differentiate the two, as they often begin to blur. Summative assessments may be given before the end of a unit, leaving time for modification in instruction and time for student revision. Moreover, teachers are constantly assessing to see where students are in respect to goals. If they keep careful records of some of these regular assessments, they can be used to inform instruction and communicate with parents and the student in a more "summative" way.

The Black and Wiliam review cites evidence that ongoing assessments by teachers, combined with appropriate feedback to students, can have powerful, positive effects on student learning and achievement. They also report that the learning gains from systematic attention to formative assessment are larger than most of those found for any other educational interventions. Although such findings provide impressive evidence of classroom practices that really work in improving student understanding, they also report that such practices are currently underdeveloped in most classrooms.

Black and Wiliam also offer a cautionary comment: Although many features essential to fruitful development of formative assessment now can be identified, there is no single, simple recipe that teachers could adopt and follow. Even though they differ from one another in many of the details, a variety of approaches to enhancing formative assessment turn out to be successful in improving learning. Why? Teachers differ and so do their students. The opportunities provided

in various schools for engaging in an active science program differ as well.

Similarly many theories have been proposed as guides to improving learning, and several of them have practical implications. Many of the classroom-assessment examples in this volume emphasize the social and community aspects of learning. Learning is not viewed as solely an individual activity. For example, teachers and students develop shared understandings of standards for quality work and certain kinds of feedback extend and deepen these understandings. Other theories of learning highlight somewhat different aspects: meta-cognition (thinking about thinking) (Hacker, Dunlosky, & Graesser, 1998), "zones of proximal development" (deepening understanding by probing accessible knowledge for which one is prepared and ready) (Vygotsky, 1962); and the related idea that the teacher's role is to provide "scaffolding" for learning (an intellectual framework to which new ideas might be related) (Wood, Bruner, & Ross, 1976). There also are suggestive practices associated with the concept of "self-regulated" learning in which personal attributes and opportunities to learn intersect (Schunk & Zimmerman, 1998).

## A FRAMEWORK FOR FORMATIVE ASSESSMENT

Notwithstanding the differing conceptions and views about learning, all the best uses of formative assessment in the classroom seem to have a single common and straightforward underpinning that is fundamental to good educational practice. All these theories of learning—and several others—are consistent with the teacher helping the student operate within a framework of three guiding questions:

1. Where are you trying to go? (identify and communicate the learning and performance goals);
2. Where are you now? (assess, or help the student to self-assess, current levels of understanding);
3. How can you get there? (help the student with strategies and skills to reach the goal).

Almost all the theories that bear on formative assessment in the classroom can be related to this framework. The main point here, however, is that assessment (the second point) linked to action (the third point) results in formative assessment (Sadler, 1989).

Of course, it is not always necessary or even possible to follow these steps in a formal or sequential way when actually teaching. In the usual give-and-take of classroom life, opportunities arise unexpectedly to reexamine the goal of learning, to revisit a student's current understanding of a concept, and to revise the path toward the goal.

## Science Content

This three-step guideline also leads to the centrality of a feature that underlies all three questions: the science content. The improvement of **science education** is the goal of the *Standards*, but much of what has been said so far in this chapter relates to any subject, not specifically science. Yet the formative assessment process cannot be implemented well in any field of study without serious attention to the nature and level of the subject matter to be taught. Which concepts are most important and for what reasons? Are some ideas particularly fruitful for laying the foundations for further learning? Are some of them more closely related than others to what the students already know, and thus can be presumed to be more accessible? In choosing a main content goal and the associated intermediate goals, which may be stepping-stones toward understanding that goal, the **science teacher** will be exercising subject expertise by: committing to certain **aims** for learning science, knowing the **science concepts** that best relate to that goal, and by **professional understanding** of the ways by which students may make progress in understanding the concepts and skills that lead to those goals. Furthermore, the choice of ways to assess student work similarly will be guided by personal **pedagogical** knowledge of those obstacles that are commonly encountered by students in learning the particular science concepts that are chosen. These important responsibilities and daily decisions regarding curriculum and assessment underscore the importance of science teachers having a solid background and understanding of the science subject matter that they teach.

## THE TEACHER'S ROLE

Much of the responsibility for implementing the science standards rests with classroom teachers. Assessment is no exception. The *Standards* recognize the importance of a teacher's ongoing assessments and indicate that classroom teachers are in the position to best use assessment in powerful ways for both formative and summative purposes, including improving classroom practice, planning curricula, developing self-directed learners, reporting student progress, and investigating their own teaching practices. Teachers' participation in classroom activities, hour after hour, day after day, positions them to gain information and insight into their students' understandings, actions, interests, intentions, and motivation that would be difficult to glean from tests (Darling-Hammond, 1994; Moss, 1994, 1996). Teachers need not only to interpret the assessment-generated information, they also must use the information to adapt their teaching repertoires to the needs of their students.

## Feedback—Cognitive and Affective

The usefulness and effectiveness of formative assessment depend, in part, on the quality and saliency of the information gathered in the first place and the appropriateness and relevance of subsequent actions. The quality of the feedback rather than its existence or absence is the central point (Bangert-Downs, Kulik, Kulik, & Morgan, 1991; Sadler, 1989).

With regard to feedback, research makes the case for the use of descriptive, criterion-based feedback as opposed to numerical scoring or letter grades without clear criteria (Butler & Neuman, 1995; Cameron & Pierce, 1994; Kluger & deNisi, 1996). For example, in a study conducted by Butler (1987) with a random sampling of students, individuals completed an assessment task and then received one of three types of feedback: (a) tailored, written remarks addressing criteria they were aware of before taking the assessment, (b) grades derived from scoring of previous work, or (c) both grades and comments. Scores on two subsequent tasks increased most significantly for those who received detailed comments, while scores declined for those who received both comments and grades. For those assigned grades only, scores declined and then increased between the second and third tasks.

Butler's research is important to

consider in light of current research in attribution theory (Skaalvik, 1990; Vispoel & Austin, 1995). Research shows that feedback that emphasizes learning goals leads to greater learning gains than feedback that emphasizes self-esteem (Ames, 1992; Butler, 1988; Dweck, 1986). With respect to feedback emphasizing self-esteem, high-performing students often attribute their performance to effort and low-performing students attribute their performance to lack of ability (Butler & Newman, 1995; Cameron & Pierce, 1994; Kluger & deNisi, 1996). Students who repeatedly receive a grade of C– often believe that a C– is all that they are capable of achieving. Comments can take the focus from such attribution of success, or lack thereof, to the quality of the work at hand and areas where it can be strengthened. While grades can sometimes contribute to a competitive classroom environment where performance is normative (judged in relation to that of peers), comments that attend to specified criteria for higher quality work can help provide students with the feedback they need to develop their understanding and make progress.

Although letter grades are the most prevalent form of feedback, Stiggins (2001) reminds educators that grades serve as a way to convey a lot of information as a symbol for ease in communication. The symbol, or letter, can be only as meaningful as the definitions of achievement that underpin them and the quality of the assessment that produced them.

## Design, Selection, and Participation

To use ongoing assessment to best facilitate student growth, the teacher plays a key role in choosing and organizing student tasks in ways that encourage them to speak and write so as to elicit their levels of understanding. Although almost any sample of student work can provide an occasion for a rich assessment discussion and can provide the teacher with assessment information, teachers also **plan** for opportunities for students to discuss and display their levels of understanding. They also create situations and allocate time for students to examine and discuss guidelines for high-quality work. These tasks are demanding ones and are discussed further in Chapters 3 and 5.

The *Standards* promote greater emphasis on teachers "continuously assessing student understanding," on "assessing rich, well-structured knowledge," on "assessing scientific understanding and reasoning," on "students engaged in ongoing assessment of their work and that of others," and on "teachers [becoming] involved in the development of external assessments" (p. 100).

The point of this last emphasis is significant: The *Standards* seek to extend a teacher's influence beyond the classroom, or even the school, by advocating active teacher involvement in the **development and interpretation** of externally designed assessment used primarily for accountability purposes. Recent reforms in several state-assessment policies and practices in other countries provide models of how a teacher's assessments and participation can become more integral to the external assessments. This topic is discussed in Chapters 4, 5, and 6. Teacher involvement at this level is important to consider for many reasons, not the least of which is the centrality of inquiry in the vision of science education advanced in the *Standards*. Inquiry is difficult to assess in a one-time test. A teacher's position in the classroom allows for personal judgments of one's abilities over an extended investigation that cannot be matched by any feasible external testing procedure.

## THE STUDENT'S ROLE

Student participation in the assessment process becomes essential if the *Standards* are to be actualized for all students. Specifically, **self**-assessment becomes crucial for feedback to be used effectively. Students are the ones who must ultimately take action to bridge the gap between where they are and where they are heading (Sadler, 1989). Brown (1994) stresses the strategic element of being aware of

particular strengths and weaknesses: "Effective learners operate best when they have insight into their own strengths and weaknesses and access to their own repertoires of strategies for learning" (p. 9).

Research shows the potential learning gains from engaging students in peer- and self-assessment strategies (Covington, 1992; Darling-Hammond, Ancess, & Falk, 1995; White & Frederiksen, 1998; Wolf, Bixby, Glen, & Gardner, 1991). In a controlled experiment in two middle school science classrooms, White and Frederiksen (1998) demonstrated increases in student achievement in the class where discussion was structured to promote reflective peer- and self-assessment. The control group participated in general discussions of the curriculum content for the same amount of time but did not show the same increase in student achievement. Traditionally low-attaining students demonstrated the most notable improvement. This last point should not be overlooked. Supporting all students in their quest for high performance in science is an underlying principle of the science education standards. As this research indicates, assessment can be a critical means of reaching the goal.

Although the White and Frederiksen study demonstrates improved performance with regular student self-reflection, involving students in the assessment process can serve other purposes as well. In a year-long teacher-researcher collaborative project in an elementary classroom, Rudd and Gunstone (1993) helped foster self-assessment skills through questionnaires, concept maps, and self-assessment maps. The researchers cite the following as evidence of an enhanced learning environment:

- the development of students' abilities to plan and think through their goals and skills;
- the creation of student awareness of the importance of evaluating their own work;
- the students' abilities to evaluate each other's self-assessment and in then providing constructive criticism; and
- the students' abilities to manage resources and time more effectively.

Assessment provides opportunities to discuss and develop a common understanding of what constitutes quality work. Students can have substantive conversations about what constitutes a good lab investigation, a salient scientific response, an appropriate use of evidence, or an effective presentation. Such discussions can be preliminary to the difficult challenge of trying to develop detailed assessment rubrics—tools that provide detailed descriptions and criteria for varying performance levels used to assess student work or responses—to help gauge quality work in each of these dimensions and to help guide

the production of quality work. Participating in assessment can provide students with opportunities to reflect on what they are learning in order to make coherent connections within and between subject matters (Cole, Coffey, & Goldman, 1999; Resnick & Resnick, 1991; Wiggins, 1998). In the process of such deliberation, students often generate many of the salient educational goals themselves (Duschl & Gitomer, 1997). The process increases their commitment to achieving them (Covington, 1992). Furthermore, the ability to self-assess is essential for becoming a self-directed, lifelong learner (NRC, 1996), one of the aims set forth in the *Standards*.

## THE SCHOOL'S ROLE

In-depth case studies conducted by Darling-Hammond and colleagues (1995) report how teachers and students in five schools used assessment to inform instruction and stimulate greater learning. Their work reinforces that assessment that makes learning central cannot be separated from other aspects of schooling. By focusing on schools where assessment occurs through "real-world" challenges that engage students in the assessment process, the studies provide examples of the role that observation, logs, portfolios, journal writing, and self- and peer-assessment, can play in facilitating powerful learning.

Portfolios (collections of student

work), regular self-reflection and peer assessment, assessment conversations, journals, projects, class discussions, performances, well-planned quizzes and tests—any combination of these assessment activities—can support improved science learning. In many classrooms, teachers are engaged in powerful teaching practices where assessment and learning work in concert toward creating a meaningful learning environment that benefits all students. However, another message that comes across in Darling-Hammond's case-study work is that many other teachers face school, district, or state policies that thwart attempts to move toward the vision of assessment and learning set forth in the *Standards*. Therefore, ensuring that assessment supports student learning requires support throughout the entire educational system. The system level is the topic of Chapter 6.

## ASSESSMENT AND HIGH STANDARDS

A major impetus behind the standards movement is the expectation that **all** students are to achieve the high standards. To reach that goal, greater attention to classroom assessment that supports learning becomes particularly compelling, and teachers and researchers need to focus attention on how classroom assessment can be used as a means to this end. Assessment tools that calculate solely how well student achievement measures up to the standards, however reliable, will not suffice. Table 2-1 outlines the changes that are relevant to formative assessment as stated in the *Standards* (p. 100). Assessment also must serve as a vehicle for **improving** the quality of learning for every student. There is a clear and indivisible connection among assessment, curriculum, and teaching.

## TABLE 2-1 Changing Emphases of Assessment

| Less Emphasis On | More Emphasis On |
|---|---|
| Assessing what is easily measured | Assessing what is most highly valued |
| Assessing discrete knowledge | Assessing rich, well-structured knowledge |
| Assessing scientific knowledge | Assessing scientific understanding and reasoning |
| Assessing to learn what students do not know | Assessing to learn what students understand |
| End-of-term assessments by teachers | Students engaged in ongoing assessment of their work and that of others |
| Development of external assessments by measurement experts alone | Teachers involved in the development of external assessments |

SOURCE: NRC. (1996).

Although the availability and intelligent use of curriculum and materials is essential, as Darling-Hammond (1994) suggests, "[e]fforts to raise standards of learning and performance must rest in part on strategies to transform assessment" (p. 6).

## MULTIPLE PURPOSES OF ASSESSMENT

Although responsibility for assessment falls to the entire educational system, teachers and students are the primary designers, collectors, and users of assessment data in the direct service of learning. Recognizing the unique position of the classroom teacher, the science standards seek to recognize, legitimate, and extend the purview of the teacher in a range of assessment purposes and practices. In a comprehensive and coherent assessment system, teachers must accommodate the range of purposes that classroom assessment must serve—from self-reflection on practice, to monitoring achievement for individual students and assigning grades, to gauging levels of engagement, to reporting to parents, to making decisions about the placement of students. Black (1997) categorizes the **purposes** of assessment into those concerned with (a) support of learning; (b) certification, which includes reporting individual achievement, or grading, placement and promotion; and (c) accountability. Table 2-2 presents a visual overview that highlights the distinctions among the types, purposes, and locus of influence, as well as who takes on the primary roles and responsibilities with respect to the assessment.

Because different people are making judgments about students for different purposes, there are often serious areas of overlap that lead to ambiguities and tensions. Teachers, for example, must balance their roles

**TABLE 2-2 Types, Purposes, and Roles and Responsibilities for Assessment**

| Type | Purpose | Roles and Responsibilities |
|---|---|---|
| Formative | Improve learning<br>Inform instruction | Student and teacher |
| Summative | Grading<br>Placement<br>Promotion | Teachers and external tests |
|  | Accountability | External tests (and teacher) |

as facilitator and coach to promote learning along with their role as judge when they assign grades at the end of the term. External assessors, who prepare the standardized tests, serve primarily a summative function. It is important to keep in mind the different uses of assessment, the people who have the major responsibilities for them, and the intended audience, especially when considering the mechanisms employed to collect evidence and the inferences drawn from the collected data. For teachers especially, because they must engage in both formative and summative assessment practices, it is necessary to identify and attempt to mitigate the existing tensions. The challenge for classroom teachers becomes one of recognizing the range of factors that constitute assessment activity and taking full advantage of them to advance curricular, instructional, and learning goals. The challenge for the system becomes one of providing teachers and their students with the structures and necessary support to do so. These challenges are further elaborated in the chapters that follow.

## KEY POINTS

• Research shows that regular and high-quality formative assessment can have a powerful, positive effect on student learning and achievement. The achievement gains associated with systematic attention to formative assessment are greater than most other educational interventions.

• The *Standards* indicate that classroom teachers are in the position to best use assessment in powerful ways for both formative and summative purposes, including improving classroom practice, planning curricula, developing self-directed learners, reporting student progress, and investigating their own teaching practices.

• There is no single recipe or blueprint that all teachers can successfully adopt and follow.

• Student participation in assessment becomes essential if high standards are to be actualized for all students.

• Assessment tools that calculate solely how well student achievement measures up to the standards, however reliable, will not suffice. Assessment must serve as a vehicle for improving the quality of learning for every student.

• Teachers need support from the larger system to realize and to take advantage of the possibilities of good assessment.

# 3
# Assessment in the Classroom

The primary audiences for this chapter are classroom teachers and teacher educators. The chapter offers a guiding framework to use when considering everyday assessments and then discusses the roles and responsibilities of teachers and students in improving assessment. Administrators also may be interested in the material presented in this chapter.

Assessment usually conjures up images of an end-of-unit test, a quarterly report card, a state-level examination on basic skills, or the letter grade for a final laboratory report. However, these familiar aspects of assessment do not capture the full extent or subtlety of how assessment operates every day in the classroom. The type of classroom assessment discussed in this chapter focuses upon the daily opportunities and interactions afforded to teachers and students for collecting information about student work and understandings, then uses that information to improve both teaching and learning. It is a natural part of classroom life that is a world away from formal examinations—both in spirit and in purpose.

During the school day, opportunities often arise for producing useful assessment information for teachers and students. In a class discussion, for example, remarks by some of the students may lead the teacher to believe that they do not understand the concept of energy conservation. The teacher decides that the class will revisit an earlier completed laboratory activity and, in the process, examine the connections between that activity and the discussion at hand. As groups of students conduct experiments, the teacher circulates around the room and questions individuals about the conclusions drawn from their data.

The students have an opportunity to reflect on and demonstrate their thinking. By trying to identify their sources of evidence, the teacher better understands where their difficulties arise and can alter their teaching accordingly and lead the students toward better understanding of the concept.

As another example, a planning session about future science projects in which the students work in small groups on different topic issues leads to a discussion about the criteria for judging the work quality. This type of assessment discussion, which occurs before an activity even starts, has a powerful influence on how the students conduct themselves throughout the activity and what they learn. During a kindergarten class discussion to plan a terrarium, the teacher recognizes that one of the students confuses rocks for living organisms and yet another seems unclear about the basic needs of plants. So the conversation is turned toward these topics to clarify these points. In this case, classroom teaching is reshaped immediately as a result of assessments made of the students' understanding.

Abundant assessment opportunities exist in each of these examples. Indeed, Hein and Price (1994) assert that anything a student does can be used for assessment purposes. This means there is no shortage of opportunities, assessment can occur at any time. One responsibility of the teacher is to use meaningful learning experiences as meaningful assessment experiences. Another is to select those occasions particularly rich in potential to teach something of importance about standards for high-quality work. To be effective as assessment that improves teaching and learning, the information generated from the activity must be used to inform the teacher and/or students in helping to decide what to do next. In such a view, assessment becomes virtually a continuous classroom focus, quite indistinguishable from teaching and curriculum.

The *Standards* convey a view of assessment and learning as two sides of the same coin and essential for all students to achieve a high level of understanding in science. To best support their students' learning, teachers are continuously engaged in ongoing assessments of the learning and teaching in their classroom. An emphasis on formative assessment—assessment that informs teaching and learning and occurs throughout an activity or unit—is incorporated into regular practice. Furthermore, teachers cultivate this integrated view of teaching, learning, and continuous assessment among their students. When formative assessment becomes an integral part of classroom practice, student achievement is enhanced (Black & Wiliam, 1998a; Crooks, 1988; Fuchs & Fuchs, 1986). However, as discussed in the previous chapter, research also indicates that this type of assessment often is not recognized as significant by teachers, principals, parents, or the general public, and is seldom articulated or featured as a priority. Box 3-1 provides definitions for "formative" and "summative," which pertain to the two main functions that assessment can take.

The centrality of inquiry in the vision of science education advanced in the *Standards* provides a particularly compelling reason to take a closer look at classroom assessment, and formative assessment, in particular. If students are to **do** science, not solely verbalize major facts and principles, they should engage in activity that extends over several days or weeks. Their work should be less episodic and fractured than lesson-based science teaching. A different kind of assessment is necessary, one that is designed to help students get better at inquiring into the world of science (NRC, 2000). The best way to support inquiry is to obtain information about students while they are actually engaged in science investigations with a view toward helping them develop their understandings of both subject matter and procedure. The information collected by teachers and students while the students are at work can be used to guide their progress. A teacher asks questions that may help spur thinking about science concepts that are part of the investigation and may help students understand what it takes to do work that comports with high standards. At the end, the information may be collected and reviewed to form a basis for summative evaluations.

## FEATURES OF FORMATIVE ASSESSMENT

To help design and implement an effective and efficient classroom assessment system, we offer the following general template for designing and integrating formative assessment into regular classroom practice.

- **Where are you trying to go?**
- **Where are you now?**
- **How can you get there?**

Having posed these questions as a guide, it is important to note that no one blueprint or single best model exists for using assessment as a tool that, first and foremost, supports and facilitates student learning. Each teacher needs to develop a system that works for him or her. By making explicit desirable features of assessment, these three critical questions provide a framework for achieving powerful classroom assessment. The questions and the obtained responses are tightly interconnected and interdependent and they are not new. Based on experience, many teachers both intuitively and purposefully consider these questions every day. Attention to them is part of good teaching.

Through the vignettes and discussion that follow, we hope to make features of formative assessment more explicit and, in doing so, highlight how intimately they are connected to teaching.

---

### A Look Inside Two Classrooms

The seventh-grade students in Ms. K's science class are working on long-term research projects investigating their local watershed. In addition to class discussions, laboratory activities, and field trips, small groups of students are exploring various areas of particular interest and importance. One group is surveying local industrial, agricultural, and residential areas to locate general and point sources of pollutants. Another group is examining water quality. A third group is focusing on how the local ecosystem influences water quality. During project work-time, Ms. K conducts conferences with groups of students about their projects. In these small groups, the students share the details of their project; from content to process, Ms. K keeps herself informed on the working status of the different groups. Information she gathers from these conferences feeds into her decisions about allotment of work time, possible resource suggestions, and areas where she can identify additional learning opportunities. She also is able to note progress that occurs throughout the project, as well as from the last time she engaged in a similar activity with students. For example, after one of the discussions, she realized that the students in one group were not connecting algal blooms to possible sources of pollutants. She asked questions that encouraged them to explore possible causes of the burst in algal blooms, and together they devised an experiment that had the potential of providing them with some useful, additional information.

Journals kept by the students become the stimulus for regular reflections on learning and the connections between their topic to the bigger picture of the local watershed. Ms. K collects the journals weekly. The journal reflections inform her about the progress of the groups and the difficulties they are having, and so serve as a springboard for class discussion. From reading student responses and listening to discussion, Ms. K knows that some of her students are making deeper connections, and many are making different connections. Painting the broad landscape for the entire class will give those who are struggling to find a broader context for their work and sustain their inquiries, so she decides to create an opportunity to do so. When she is not in discussions with students, she mills around the areas where her students work, moving from group to group, sometimes asking questions, sometimes just listening and observing before she joins the next group. She carries a clipboard on which she jots down notes, quotes, and questions that she will want to come back to with a particular student or the entire group. Through the journals, her observations, the discussions, and other assessment activities, Ms. K stays connected to the sense her students are making of their work as it unfolds.

At the very beginning of the project, Ms. K and her students started conversations about how their projects would be assessed. As a class, they cycle back through the criteria that were established, deepening understanding by highlighting exemplars from past projects and just talking through what constitutes quality work. They share examples of visual display boards, written reports, and models from other projects. Ms. K wants to make sure that each student understands the standards that they are expected to meet. Students chose many of the criteria by which they wish their peers to evaluate them, and, with Ms. K's help, they developed an evaluation rubric that will be ready on presentation day—now just 2 weeks away. At that time, they will be making public reports to peers, parents, and community members.

SOURCE: Coffey (2001).

■ ■ ■

The King School was reforming its science curriculum. After considerable research into existing curriculum materials and much discussion, the team decided to build a technology piece into some of the current science studies. The third-grade teacher on the team, Ms. R., said that she would like to work with two or three of her colleagues on the third-grade science curriculum. They selected three topics that they knew they would be teaching the following year: life cycles, sound, and water.

Ms. R. chose to introduce technology as part of the study of sound. That winter, when the end of the sound study neared, Ms. K., was ready with a new culminating activity—making musical instruments. She posed a question to the entire class: Having studied sound for almost 6 weeks, could they design and make musical instruments that would produce sounds for entertainment? Ms. R had collected a variety of materials, which she now displayed on a table, including boxes, tubes, string, wire, hooks, scrap wood, dowels, plastic, rubber, fabric and more. The students had been working in groups of four during the sound study, and Ms. R asked them to gather into those groups to think about the kinds of instruments they would like to make. Ms. R asked the students to think particularly about what they knew about sound, what kind of sound they would like their instruments to make, and what kind of instrument it would be. How would the sound be produced? What would make the sound? She suggested they might want to look at the materials she had brought in, but they could think about other materials too.

Ms. R sent the students to work in their groups. Collaborative work had been the basis of most of the science inquiry the student had done; for this phase, Ms. R felt that the students should work together to discuss and share ideas, but she suggested that each student might want to have an instrument at the end to play and to take home.

As the students began to talk in their groups, Ms. R added elements to the activity. They would have only the following 2 weeks to make their instruments. Furthermore, any materials they needed beyond what was in the boxes had to be materials that were readily available and inexpensive.

Ms. R. knew that planning was a challenge for these third graders. She moved among groups, listening and adding comments. When she felt that discussions had gone as far as they could go, she asked each group to draw a picture of the instruments the children thought they would like to make, write a short piece on how they thought they would make them, and make a list of the materials that they would need. Ms. R made a list of what was needed, noted which children and which groups might profit from discussing their ideas with one another, and suggested that the children think about their task, collect materials if they could, and come to school in the next week prepared to build their instruments.

Ms. R. invited several sixth graders to join the class during science time the following week, knowing that the third-grade students might need their help in working with the materials. Some designs were simple and easy to implement, for example, one group was making a rubber-band player by stretching different widths and lengths of rubber bands around a plastic gallon milk container with the top cut off. Another group was making drums of various sizes using some thick cardboard tubes and pieces of thin rubber roofing material. For many, the designs could not be translated into reality, and much change and trial and error ensued. One group planned to build a guitar and designed a special shape for the sound box, but after the glued sides of their original box collapsed twice, the group decided to use the wooden box that someone had added to the supply table. In a few cases, the original design was abandoned, and a new design emerged as the instrument took shape.

At the end of the second week, Ms. R set aside 2 days for the students to reflect on what they had done individually and as a class. On Friday, they were once again to draw and write about their instruments. Where groups had worked together on an instrument, one report was to be prepared. On the next Monday, each group was to make a brief presentation of the instrument, what it could do, how the design came to be, and what challenges had been faced. As a final effort, the class could prepare a concert for other third grades.

In making the musical instruments, students relied on knowledge and understanding developed while studying sound, as well as the principles of design, to make an instrument that produced sound. The assessment task for the musical instruments follows. The titles emphasize some important components of the assessment process.

**Science Content:**  The K-4 science content standard on science and technology is supported by the idea that students should be able to communicate the purpose of a design.  The K-4 physical science standard is supported by the fundamental understanding of the characteristics of sound, a form of energy.

**Assessment Activity:**  Students demonstrate the products of their design work to their peers and reflect on what the project taught them about the nature of sound and the process of design.

**Assessment Type:**  This can be public, group, or individual, embedded in teaching.

**Assessment Purpose:**  This activity assesses student progress toward understanding the purpose and processes of design.  The information will be used to plan the next design activity.  The activity also permits the teacher to gather data about understanding of sound.

**Data:**  Observations of the student performance.

**Context:**  Third-grade students have not completed a design project.  Their task is to present the product of their work to their peers and talk about what they learned about sound and design as a result of doing the project.  This is a challenging task for third-grade students, and the teacher will have to provide considerable guidance to the groups of students as they plan their presentations.

As described in the science standards, the teacher provided the following directions that served as a framework that students could use to plan their presentations.

1. Play your instrument for the class.
2. Show the class the part of the instrument that makes the sound.
3. Describe to the class the purpose (function) that the other parts of the instrument have.
4. Show the class how you can make the sound louder.
5. Show the class how you can change the pitch (how high or how low the sound is) of the sound.
6. Tell the class about how you made the instrument, including
   • What kind of instrument did you want to make?
   • How like the instrument you wanted to make is the one you actually made?
   • Why did you change your design?
   • What tools and materials did you use to make your instrument?
7. Explain why people make musical instruments.

In order to evaluate the student performance, the teacher used the following guidelines:

Student understanding of sound will be revealed by understanding that the sound is produced in the instrument by the part of the instrument that vibrates (moves rapidly back and forth), that the pitch (how high or how low) can be changed by changing how rapidly the vibrating part moves, and the loudness can be changed by the force (how hard you pluck, tap, or blow the vibrating part) with which the vibrating part is set into motion.  An average student performance would include the ability to identify the source of the vibration and ways to change either pitch or loudness in two directions (raise and lower the pitch of the instrument or make the instrument louder and softer) or change the pitch and loudness in one direction (make the pitch higher and the sound louder). An exemplary performance by a student would include not only the ability to identify the source of the vibration but also to change pitch and loudness in both directions.

Student understanding of the nature of technology will be revealed by the student's ability to reflect on why people make musical instruments—to improve the quality of life—as well as by their explanations of how they managed to make the instrument despite the constraints faced—that is, the ability to articulate why the conceptualization and design turned out to be different from the instrument actually made. (p. 49)

SOURCE: NRC (1996).

---

There is no one best assessment system for the classroom. What works for Ms. K or Ms. R in their classrooms may not work in another. What is important is that assessment is an ongoing activity, one that relies on multiple strategies and sources for collecting information that bears on the quality of student work and that then can be used to help both the students and the teacher think more pointedly about how the quality might be improved.

In the first vignette, Ms. K is helping her students by painting the broad landscape so that they can see how their work fits into a wider context. She also reminds them of the criteria for quality work. Thus, she is helping them to develop a clear view of what they are to achieve and where they are going. At this stage, the view is usually clearer to the teacher than to the students. One of her responsibilities is to help the students under-

stand and share the goals, which will become progressively clearer to them as the inquiry progresses.

To chart student progress, Ms. K relies on several strategies and sources: observations, conversations, journal assignments, student work, and a final presentation. These opportunities are part of the natural flow of classroom life, indistinguishable for her and for the students from collecting data, discussing findings, planning next steps, drawing conclusions, and communicating findings about the main concepts they are expected to learn. In helping her students to reach their goal, she bases her actions on multiple pieces of evidence that she gleans from activities embedded in her teaching and curriculum. She uses this information to make decisions about work time, about support she needs to provide, and about resource suggestions.

Ms. R also uses assessment in

strategic and productive ways. She frames an assessment task in a way that will engage students to learn as they prepare for the final presentation and concert. Peer-design reviews, conversations, and other assessments were built into the activity of designing and building instruments so that students could draw from these to inform their design and construction of instruments. She provides the students with prompts and elements that should be included in their presentations so that the students will be clear on what is required. She has clear guidelines about the quality and depth of responses in terms of how students will demonstrate their understandings and skills.

The usefulness of assessment does not stop at teachers collecting information in the course of their teaching and providing feedback. Like Ms. K and Ms. R, they plan and structure specific assessment events, such as individual conferences with students, occasions for the students to write about a topic, design reviews, observations of students at work, presentations of work, and initiating whole-class discussion of what they have learned so far. These are just some of the many assessment activities and methods available to teachers and students. In these same scenarios, teachers could also have integrated the use of additional written assessments—including selected response, short answer, essay, lab reports, homework problems, among

others—into their teaching in ways that would generate rich assessment opportunities.

Throughout this text, we have attempted to avoid technical terms whenever possible. When we do use them, we try to offer a definition or use it in a context where its meaning makes sense. Box 3-2 provides

## BOX 3-2  Assessment Terms

**Alternative assessment:**
   Asessments that are different in form than traditional paper-and-pencil assessments.

**Performance assessment:**
   Asessments that allow students to demonstrate their understandings and skills (to a teacher or an outsider) as they perform a certain activity. They are evaluated by a teacher or an outsider on the quality of their ability to perform specific tasks and the products they create in the process.

**Portfolio assessment:**
   A purposeful and representative collection of student work that conveys a story of progress, achievement and/or effort. The student is involved in selecting pieces of work and includes self-reflections of what understandings the piece of work demonstrates. Thus, criteria for selection and evaluation need to be made clear prior to selection.

**Embedded assessment:**
   Asessments that occur as part of regular teaching and curricular activities.

**Authentic assessment:**
   Asessments that require students to perform complex tasks representative of activities actually done in out-of-school settings.

operational definitions of several terms you will find in the assessment literature.

Now, consider the assessment in the two vignettes in light of the following three guiding questions: Where are you trying to go? Where are you now? How can you get there?

## WHERE ARE YOU TRYING TO GO?

### Clear Criteria

The goals articulated in the *Standards* arise from their emphasis on the active nature of science and their stress on the range of activities that encompass what it means to do science and to understand both specific concepts and the subject area as a whole. Thus, the *Standards* advocate going beyond the coverage of basic facts to include skills and thought processes, such as the ability to ask questions, to construct and test explanations of phenomena, to communicate ideas, to work with data and use evidence to support arguments, to apply knowledge to new situations and new questions, to problem solve and make decisions, and to understand history and nature of scientific knowledge (NRC, 1996). To best assist students in their science learning, assessment should attend to these many facets of learning, including content understanding, application, processes, and reasoning.

In his book on classroom assessment for teachers, Stiggins (2001) writes,

> The quality of any assessment depends first and foremost on the clarity and appropriateness of our definitions of the achievement target to be assessed…We cannot assess academic achievement effectively if we do not know and understand what that valued target is. (p. 19)

As Stiggins states, it is important that teachers have clear performance criteria in mind before they assess student work and responses. Ms. R's guidelines included attention to both: she expected her students to demonstrate an understanding of concepts of sound, such as causes of pitch, as well as the nature of technology. Before the students engaged in the assessment, Ms. R had outlined how she would evaluate the student responses in each area.

Clarity about the overall goals is only a first step. Given that goals are clear, the teacher has to help the students achieve greater clarity. This usually entails identification of somewhat discrete stages that will help the students to understand what is required to move toward the goal. These intermediate steps often emerge as the study progresses, often in lesson design and planning but also on the spot in the classroom as information about the students' levels of understanding become clearer, new special interests become apparent, or unexpected learning difficulties arise. This complex, pedagogical challenge is heightened because the goals that embody the standards and the related criteria need to be understood by **all** students.

One of the goals of the *Standards* is for all students to become independent lifelong learners. The standards emphasize the integral role that regular self-assessment plays in achieving this goal. The document states:

> Students need the opportunity to evaluate and reflect on their own scientific understanding and ability. Before students can do this, they need to understand the goals for learning science. The ability to self-assess understanding is an essential tool for self-directed learning. (p. 88)

Sadler (1989) emphasizes the importance of student understanding of what constitutes quality work, "The indispensable condition for improvement is that the student comes to hold a concept of quality roughly equivalent to that held by the teacher..." (p. 121). Yet, conveying to students the standards and criteria for good work is one of the most difficult aspects of involving them in their own assessment. Again, teachers can use various ways to help students develop and cultivate these insights. Following the example of Ms. K's class in the first vignette, students and teachers can become engaged in a substantive, assessment conversation about what is a good presentation, such as a good lab

investigation or a good reading summary while engaging students in the development process of assessment rubrics. Another starting point for these conversations could be a discussion about exemplary pieces of work, where students need to think about and share the characteristics of the piece of work that makes it "good."

In the first vignette, Ms. K facilitates frequent conversations with her class about what constitutes good work. Although these discussions occur at the beginning of the project period, she regularly and deliberately cycles back to issues of expectations and quality to increase their depth of understanding as they get more involved in their projects. In discussions of an exemplary piece of work, she encourages the students to become as specific as possible. Over time, the students begin to help refine some of the criteria by which they will be evaluated. Such a process not only helps to make the criteria more useful; it increases their ownership of the standards by which judgments will be made about their work. For her third graders, Ms. R provides guidelines for planning and presenting their instruments and introduces questions for the students to address as they engage in their work.

## WHERE ARE YOU NOW?

Once they have clearly determined where they want to go, teachers and students need to find out where students currently stand in relation to the goals. Of course, the process is not quite so linear. It is not unusual for the goals to change somewhat as the students and teachers get more involved in the study.

## Variety Is Essential

Ms. K's and Ms R's classrooms demonstrate the many ways assessment information can be obtained. In the first scenario, conferences with students allow Ms. K to ask questions, hear specifics of project activity, and probe student reasoning and thought processes. She can get a sense of how and where the individuals are making contributions to their group's work and help to ensure that they share the work at hand, including development of an understanding of the underlying processes and content addressed by the activity. The information she learns as a result of these conferences will guide decisions on time allocation, pace, resources, and learning activities that she can help provide. After observations and listening to students discuss instruments, Ms. R made the judgment that her students were ready to continue with the activity. The journals prepared by Ms. K's students and the individual reflections of Ms. R's provided the teachers with an indication of their understanding of the scientific concepts they were working with, and thereby allowed them to gain

new and different insights into their respective students' work. The entries also provided the teachers with a mechanism, though not the only one, to gain some insight into the individual student's thinking, understanding, and ability to apply knowledge. In Ms. K's class, the journal writing was regular enough that the teacher's comments and questions posed in response to the entries could guide the students as they revisit previous work and move on to related activities and reflections.

Through such varied activities, the teachers in the vignettes are able to see how the students make sense of the data, the context into which they place the data, as well as the opportunity to evaluate and then assist the students on the ability to articulate their understandings and opinions in a written format or by incorporating understandings into a design. As they walk around the room, listening, observing, and interacting with students, both teachers take advantage of the data they collect.

Any single assessment is not likely to be comprehensive enough to provide high-quality information in all the important areas so that a student or teacher can make use of the data. Ms. K, for example, would not use the student conferences to obtain all the information she needs about student comprehension and involvement. She gets different information from reading student journals. In the individual reflections, Ms. R can get additional data to complement or reinforce the information obtained by observing students as they engage in the activity or by talking with them.

## Questioning

The occasions to sit with, converse with, question, and listen to the students gave Ms. K and Ms. R the opportunities to employ powerful questioning strategies as an assessment tool. When teachers ask salient open-ended questions and allow for an appropriate window or wait time (Rowe, 1974)—they can spur student thinking and be privy to valuable information gained from the response. Questions do not need to occur solely in whole-group discussion. The strategy can occur one-on-one as the teacher circulates around the room. Effective questioning that elicits quality responses is not easy. In addition to optimal wait-time, it requires a solid understanding of the subject matter, attentive consideration of each student's remarks, as well as skillful crafting of further leading questions. In the vignette, Ms. K needed to be aware of the existence and causes of algal blooms in order to ask questions that may lead her students down productive paths in exploring them.

## Examination of Student Work

The close examination of student work also is invaluable, and teachers do it all the time. When looking at work, it is important to ask critical questions, such as "For what does this provide evidence?" "What do they mean by this response?" "What other opportunities did the child have to demonstrate knowledge or skills?" "What future experience may help to promote further development?" "What response am I expecting?" "What are the criteria for good work?" "What are the criteria for gauging competency?" These are just a few of the questions that can spur useful analysis. Continued and careful consideration of student work can enlighten both teacher and student.

## Form to Match Purpose

Like Ms. K and Ms. R in the vignettes, teachers are not concerned with just one dimension of learning. To plan teaching and to meet their students' needs, they need to recognize if a student understands a particular concept but demonstrates difficulty in applying it in a personal investigation or if a student does not comprehend fundamental ideas underlying the concept. Specific information regarding the sources of confusions can be useful in planning activities or in initiating a conversation between students and the teacher. An array of strategies and forms of assessment to address the goals that the student and teacher have established allows students multiple opportunities to demonstrate their understandings.

This is important if we hope to support all students. Darling-Hammond (1994) comments, "if assessment is to be used to open up as many opportunities as possible to as many students as possible, it must address a wide range of talents, a variety of life experiences, and multiple ways of knowing" (p. 17).

A comprehensive understanding of science requires more than knowledge of scientific information and skills. The *Standards* articulate the breadth and depth of what it means to know and be able to do in science at different grade levels. To help ensure that assessment addresses and supports a broader view of science understanding, it can be helpful to consider the different dimensions that comprise knowledge in science. Some aspects of science knowledge are highlighted in Box 3-3.

With knowledge of the student's strengths, a teacher can help ensure that any particular assessment allows the student to demonstrate understanding and can assess whether information would be better gathered in a different format to allow for that opportunity to express thinking in different ways. For instance, Ms. K collects her assessment data from a variety of places, including discussions, conversations, conferences, observations, journals and written work, in addition to providing useful information, relying on a variety of sources and using a variety of formats so as not to privilege any one way of

## BOX 3-3 What Is "Understanding"?

Stiggins encourages teachers to devise classroom assessments of five different, but related, kinds of expectations:

1. mastery of content knowledge, where mastery includes both knowing and understanding;
2. the use of that knowledge to reason and solve problems;
3. the development of performance skills;
4. development of the ability to create products that meet certain standards of quality; and
5. the development of important dispositions.

In their work in science assessment, Shavelson and Ruiz-Primo attend to the following aspects of knowledge:

■ propositional or declarative knowledge—knowledge about facts, concepts and principles;
■ procedural knowledge—knowing how to do something; and
■ strategic knowledge—knowing which, when, and why a specific knowledge would be applicable.

They, too, stress that different forms of assessment are better suited for different aspects of knowledge.

This complexity is important to consider when developing a rich and comprehensive assessment system. Any classroom assessment system should assess and support growth in all areas. A single type or form of assessment will not be able to capture all of the dimensions of scientific knowing and doing.

SOURCE: Stiggins (2001); Shavelson and Ruiz-Primo (1999).

knowing. The conferences she sets up and the conversations that ensue give her opportunities to probe understandings and confusions and reach students that may not be as articulate when it comes to written work.

Thus the form that assessment takes is significant. The form and content of assessment should be consistent with the intended purpose. Underlying this guideline is the technical notion of validity. Technical features are discussed later in this chapter. Validity centers on whether the assessment is measuring or capturing what it is intended to measure or capture. If content understanding is the goal, it is necessary to design an appropriate assessment that would tap into that dimension of their understanding. If the ability to design an investigation is the goal, it is necessary to provide the opportunity for a student to demonstrate her ability to do such an activity. Validity is not, then, an inherent property of an individual assessment; rather, the interpretations drawn from the data and the subsequent actions that ensue are either valid or invalid. Choices for the form of the assessments are extensive and should be guided by the goals set for student learning. To find the direction for best use of the assessment data, a teacher or student gathers data in the course classroom activity by asking questions, such as "What does this information tell me?" and "How can I use it to further

learning and improve teaching?" and "What other types of data should I be looking for to help me make sense of this information?"

From Stiggins' (2001) book, *Student-Involved Classroom Assessment,* Figure 3-1 offers questions to consider when designing, selecting, or implementing an assessment. After first advising teachers to set clear and appropriate targets—or learning and performance goals—and convey these

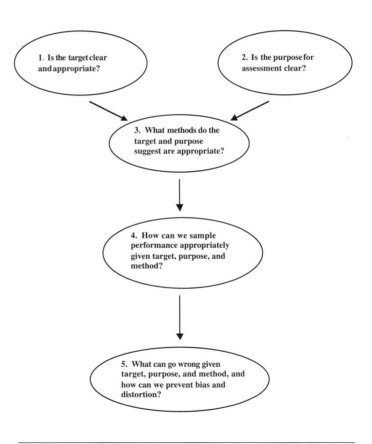

FIGURE 3-1 Considerations for designing, selecting, implementing assessment.

SOURCE: Stiggins (2001).

targets to their students, he stresses the importance of selecting appropriate methods and of taking care to avoid invalidity and bias.

## Subject-Matter Goals

Effective formative assessment must be informed by theories to ensure that it elicits the important goals of science, including a student's current understanding and procedural capability. The elements of curriculum goals and methods of instruction come together, for part of the instructor's task is to frame subgoals that are effective in guiding progress towards curriculum goals. However, this can only be done in light of the teacher's beliefs about how best to help students to learn. This introduces learning theory in addition to assessment, but in formative assessment these are very closely intertwined. Thus there has to be a conceptual analysis of the subject goals, which also is complemented by analysis of the cognitive capacities of the learners. Examples of issues that might arise are the choice between concrete but limited instances of an idea and abstract but universal presentations, the decision about whether to use daily experience or second-hand evidence, the complexity of the patterns of reasoning required in any particular approach, and research evidence about common misconceptions that hinder the progress of

students in understanding particular concepts. (For additional information on these theoretical underpinnings, see NRC, 1999a.)

Here again, depth in a teacher's subject-matter knowledge is essential. When teaching the concept of force in his high school class, Jim Minstrell is aware that although students use terms like "push" and "pull" to describe "force," the understandings they have for these terms and for the concept of force differs from those shared by scientists (Minstrell, 1992). Specifically, students often believe that a push or a pull—or a force—must be due to an active, or causal, agent. With this in mind, Minstrell carefully designs his instruction, including his questions and student experiences, to help them challenge their notions as they move towards a better understanding of the scientific phenomena and explanations involved with force. After spending time discussing and drawing the forces involved as an object is dropped to the floor, he plans questions and activities to help cultivate student understandings of more passive actions of forces so they understand that the conceptual notion of force applies to both active and passive actions and objects. His class discusses the forces involved with an object resting on a table, including the reasonableness of a table exerting an upward force. They go over other situations that would help them decide what is happening in terms of force, such as discussing the forces involved as the same object sits in the student's hand, hangs from a spring, and as the object is pushed off the edge of the table. Throughout the unit, the teacher listens carefully to his students' responses and explanations. Without an understanding of both student learning and the science involved, upon hearing the proper terms from his students, he may have proceeded with his unit with the impression that the students shared a scientific understanding of force (for a class transcript and analysis by the teacher, see Minstrell, 1992).

## Nature and Form of Feedback

The data produced from the variety of assessments illustrated in the vignettes are not only useful for the teachers but also as essential tools in helping students to realize where they stand in relation to their goals. Thus for the students, the journals with the teacher's comments added, serve as a repository for one form of feedback so they can maintain a continuing record of their work and progress. It is important to emphasize that assigning grades on a student's work does not help them to grasp what it takes on their part to understand something more accurately or deeply. Comments on a student's work that indicate specific actions to close the gap between the student's current understanding and the desired goal provide crucial help if the student takes them seriously. There is well-researched evidence that grades on student work do not help learning in the way that specific comments do. The same research shows that students generally look only at the grades and take little notice of the comments if provided (Butler, 1987). The opportunity that Ms. R's students had to design, build, and then rebuild instruments based on their trials gives them a chance to make good use of feedback to improve their piece of work.

Providing information to students is not solely a cognitive exchange. It is intertwined with issues of affect, motivation, self-esteem, self-attribution, self-concept, self-efficacy, and one's beliefs about the nature of learning. From many studies in this area (Butler, 1988; Butler & Neuman, 1995; Cameron & Pierce, 1994; Kluger & deNisi, 1996), a further generalization emerges. This is the distinction between feedback that emphasizes **learning goals** and the associated targets and feedback that focuses on **self-esteem**, often linked to the giving of grades and other reward and punishment schemes. Upon comparison of feedback in experimental studies, it is the feedback about learning goals that shows better learning gains. Feedback of the self-esteem type (trying to make the student feel better, irrespective of the quality of the work) leads less successful students to attribute their shortcomings to lack of ability. The corollary for these students is that there is little point in trying or hoping for better.

The way in which information is provided is therefore a delicate matter. Grades, and even undue praise, can reinforce expectations of failure and lead to reluctance to invest effort. Yet this culture is deeply embedded in American schools and is hard to change. This fact highlights the importance of the nature and form of the information provided to students. Thus, priority should be given to providing students with information that they can use to reach desired learning goals (Ames, 1992; Butler, 1988; Dweck, 1986).

## Timing of Assessment

In helping teachers and students establish where students stand in relation to learning goals, assessment activities are not only useful during and at the end of a unit of teaching, they also can be valuable at the start of a piece of work. Suitably open and nontechnical questions or activities can stimulate students to express how much they already know and understand about a topic. This may be particularly important when the students come from a variety of backgrounds, with some having studied aspects of the topic before, either independently or with other teachers in different schools. Such assessment can both stimulate the

thinking of the students and inform the teacher of the existing ideas and vocabularies from which the teaching has to start and on which it has to build.

## Formative Assessment in Scientific Experimentation— An Example

The following example from the Lawrence Hall of Science assessment handbook (Barber et al., 1995) demonstrates how assessment mechanisms can enrich science investigations and provide the teacher with useful information. In this illustration, students are challenged to design and conduct two experiments to determine which of three reactants—baking soda, calcium chloride, and a phenol red solution (phenol red and water)— when mixed together produces heat. The students already have completed an activity in which they mixed all three substances. The students are expected to refer to their observations and the results of that first activity. Box 3-4 illustrates a data sheet used by the students for the assessment activity, which provides prompts to record their experimental design and observations. Through this investigation, the teacher would be able to assess students' abilities to do the following:

• Design a controlled experiment in which only one ingredient is omit-

---

### BOX 3-4   Heat Experiments

**Describe your first experiment:**

What happened?

What can you conclude?

**Describe your second experiment:**

What happened?

What can you conclude?

**What do you think causes the heat?**

SOURCE:  Barber et al. (1995).

---

ted, so there is ONLY one difference between the preliminary reaction and the comparison reaction.

• Design experiments that will provide information to help determine which reactants are necessary to produce the heat in this reaction.

• Record their experiments, results, and conclusions using chemical notation as appropriate.

• Use experiment results and reasoning skills to draw conclusions about what causes heat.  (p. 152)

These students were able to arrive at some part of what would be a correct conclusion, though the degree to which the students used logical reasoning, or supported their conclu-

sions with data, varied widely.  Many came up with a correct solution but featured a noncontrol, inadequate experimental design.  In addition, the recording of results and observations was accomplished with varying degrees of clarity.  Their responses, and the language they use to describe and explain observations and phenomena, suggest varying levels of understanding of the chemical and physical changes underlying the reactions. Because the assessment was designed primarily to tap scientific investigation and experimentation skills and understandings, other assessments, including perhaps follow-up questions, would be required to make inferences about their level of conceptual understanding in the chemical and physical processes involved with these reactions.

With close examination of the student work produced in this activity, teachers were able to gain insight into abilities, skills, and understandings on which they then could provide feedback to the student. It also provided the teacher with information for additional lessons and activities on chemical and physical reactions. Boxes 3-5 through 3-9 offer samples of this type of student work along with teacher commentary.

## Creating Opportunities

Ongoing, formative assessment does not solely rely on a small-group activity structure as in the vignettes. In a whole-class discussion, teachers can create opportunities to listen carefully to student responses as they reflect on their work, an activity, or an opportunity to read aloud. In many classrooms, for example, teachers ask students to summarize the day's lesson, highlighting what sense they made of what they did. This type of format allows the teacher to hear what the students are learning from the activity and offers other students the opportunity of learning about connections that they might not have made.

In one East Palo Alto, California, classroom, the teacher asked two students at the beginning of the class to be ready to summarize their activity at the end. The class had been study-

ing DNA and had spent the class hour constructing a DNA model with colored paper representing different nucleotide bases. In their summary, the students discussed the pairing of nucleotide bases and held up their model to show how adenine pairs with thymine and cytosine pairs with guanine. Although they could identify the parts of the model and discuss the importance of "fit," they did not connect the representative pieces to a nitrogen base, sugar, and a phosphate group. When probed, they could identify deoxyribose and the phosphate group by color, but they were not able to discuss what roles these subunits played in a DNA helix. After hearing their remarks, the teacher realized that they needed help relating the generalizations from the model to an actual strand of DNA, the phenomenon they were modeling. Regardless of the format—individual, small group, whole class, project-based, written, or discussion—teachers have the opportunity to build in meaningful assessment. These opportunities should be considered in curriculum design.

## Cultivating Student Involvement in Assessment

Student participation becomes a key component of successful assessment strategies at every step: clarifying the target and purpose of assessment, discussing the assessment methods, deliberating about standards

## BOX 3-5 Sample 1: JONATHAN

**Describe your first experiment:**
C.C. + Phenol Red $\rightarrow$ heat

**What happened?**
produced heat, turned pink

**What can you conclude?**
Calcium chloride and phenol red make heat

**Describe your second experiment:**
C.C. + $H_2O$ $\rightarrow$ more heat!!

**What happened?**
produced more heat than first experiment, water turned cloudy,
calcium chloride looked dissolved

**What can you conclude?**
I conclude that the water and calcium chloride produce the most heat and the phenol red has nothing to do with making the heat, even though it got hot in the last experiment.

**What do you think causes the heat?**
I think that the water and the calcium chloride produced the heat.

**Areas for Additional Practice**
√  using scientific notation to record experiments and results

Jonathan is very systematic in his approach.  He first omits the baking soda and sees what would happen with a mixture of calcium chloride and phenol red.  Based on his results, he correctly concludes that calcium chloride and phenol make heat.  He next explores the effect of the phenol red as he substitutes water for phenol red solution and combines it with calcium chloride. He makes the astute observation that this reaction is even hotter than the calcium chloride and phenol red solution and correctly concludes that phenol red does not create the heat.  Rather, he states that water and calcium chloride produce the heat.  Jonathan uses his own abbreviation for calcium chloride, C.C. rather than $CaCO_3$, within the context of an equation format to share what ingredients were combined and the results.

SOURCE:  Barber et al. (1995).

## BOX 3-6 Sample 2: STEPHANIE

**Describe your first experiment:**
P.R. + B.S. → cold

**What happened?**
P.R. + B.S. stayed cold. Changed hot pink.

**What can you conclude?**
This mixture has nothing to do with the production of heat.

**Describe your second experiment:**
C.C. + $H_2O$ → hot

**What happened?**
The C.C. + $H_2O$ became hot.

**What can you conclude?**
This mixture provided the heat.

**What do you think causes the heat?**
The C.C. and $H_2O$ make heat for sure. It's possible that the P.R. when mixed with C.C. would cause heat, but we know that P.R. is not really a heat maker all by itself or without C.C. because of the first experiment we did. And P.R. is really a solution with water so that's another reason why water is probably what's needed, along with C.C. to make heat. We'd have to try mixing P.R. with C.C. to see if that gets hot. I think it would, but I still think that just means that water or a liquid like water is needed with C.C. to make heat.

**Areas for Additional Practice**
√   designing controlled experiments
√   using scientific notation to record experiments and results

Stephanie first decides to omit the calcium chloride and combine phenol red and baking soda. When the reaction's results are cold, she correctly concludes that this mixture has nothing to do with the production of heat. However, she does not control variables in her next experiment, when she combines calcium chloride and water. Her decision is based on the following logical, though faulty reasoning: If phenol red and baking soda do not produce heat, perhaps the other two reactants will! Technically, she should conduct another experiment so all variables are controlled. However, she considers this in her final conclusion when she discusses the possibility that mixing phenol red and calcium chloride (which she didn't try) would result in heat. She speculates on the results of this reaction, and goes on to share reasoning for her ultimate conclusion—that water, or a liquid like water, is needed with calcium chloride to make heat. Given the limitation of the two experiments, the combination she first chose, and the fact that she is aware of the weakness of her experimental design, hers is a good handling of the results. She implies that she would explore the unanswered questions if given an opportunity to conduct a third experiment. Like Jonathan, Stephanie uses chemical notation of some of her own abbreviations.

SOURCE: Barber et al. (1995).

**BOX 3-7 Sample 3: TYLER**

**Describe your first experiment:**
red stuff, CC

**What happened?**
hot pink, really hot

**What can you conclude?**
that red and CC make heat

**Describe your second experiment:**
water, baking soda, CC

**What happened?**
fizzed, hot

**What can you conclude?**
that red stuff does nothing but change color

**What do you think causes the heat?**
C.C. + water = heat

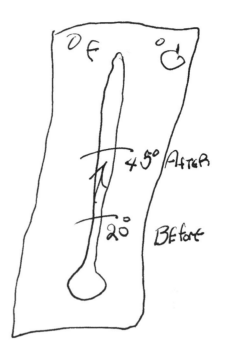

**Areas for Additional Practice**
√ keeping clear, detailed records of plans, results and conclusions
√ using scientific notation to record experiments and results

Tyler's plans, observations, and conclusions are minimally described and he refers to the phenol red as "red stuff." On the other hand, his planning and reasoning show sound scientific thinking. He first omits baking soda and determines that the phenol red and calcium chloride produce heat. For his second experiment, he removes the phenol red from the original reaction and mixes baking soda, calcium chloride and water. When this mixture also gets hot, he correctly concludes that the "red stuff" only affects the color, and therefore the calcium chloride and water produce the heat. At the end, he makes an effort at chemical notation, though he uses an equal sign (=) instead of an arrow (→ ).

SOURCE: Barber et al. (1995).

## BOX 3-8 Sample 4: EMILY

**Describe your first experiment:**
I mixed water, calcium chloride, and baking soda.

**What happened?**
It fizzed and got hot. It was hottest where the calcium chloride was.

**What can you conclude?**
The calcium chloride makes it hot.

**Describe your second experiment:**
Mixing phenol red and calcium chloride

**What happened?**
It stayed pink but it got really hot. It didn't fizz and the bag didn't inflate.

**What can you conclude?**
The calcium chloride needs a liquid to conduct heat.

**What do you think causes the heat?**
Calcium Chloride

**Areas for Additional Practice**
√ designing controlled experiments
√ drawing conclusions from experiment results
√ using scientific notation to record experiments and results

Emily substitutes water for phenol red in her first experiment. She notices the reaction is hottest near the calcium chloride and thus concludes that the calcium chloride makes it hot. This is a good hypothesis, but not a valid conclusion at this point. A more correct conclusion, based on the experiment results, is that phenol red does not cause the heat. Next, Emily combines phenol red and calcium chloride, a change of two variables in comparison to the last experiment. This new reaction also produces heat, but Emily does not conclude that baking soda is unnecessary for the heat. Rather, she states that calcium chloride needs a liquid to conduct heat. This conclusion is not based on experimental results, and it is only partially correct because aqueous liquids mixed with calcium chloride cause the heat. In addition, Emily's final conclusion (calcium chloride causes the heat) is incorrect because it omits the addition of water or a water-based liquid. She also does not use chemical notation.

SOURCE: Barber et al. (1995).

## BOX 3-9 Sample 5: KELLY

**Describe your first experiment:**
B.S. + C.C. + $H_2O$

**What happened?**
heat, bubbles, color change.

**What can you conclude?**


**Describe your second experiment:**
C.C. + phenol red solution

**What happened?**
turned hot, pink, boiled

**What can you conclude?**
Is water + C.C. or phenol + C.C.

**What do you think causes the heat?**
Water + C.C.

---

**Areas for Additional Practice**
- √ planning experiments that address a particular question
- √ designing controlled experiments
- √ keeping clear, detailed records of plans, results, and conclusions
- √ drawing conclusions from experiment results
- √ using scientific notation to record experiments and results

Kelly at first substitutes water for phenol red. Her observations of the reaction are perceptive, but she is unable to reach a conclusion. She then chooses to mix calcium chloride and phenol red solution. While technically the variables are controlled between this experiment and the original reaction—baking soda becomes the test variable—Kelly's conclusion is that water and calcium chloride, or phenol red and calcium chloride, cause the heat. These conclusions are not justified by her experiments nor is her final conclusion that water plus calcium chloride cause the heat. Her recording is minimal, though she does make an attempt to use chemical notation.

SOURCE: Barber et al. (1995).

for quality work, reflecting on the work. Sharing assessment with students does not mean that teachers transfer all responsibility to the student but rather that assessment is shaped and refined from day to day just as teaching is. For student self- and peer-assessment to be incorporated into regular practice requires cultivation and integration into daily classroom discourse, but the results can be well worth the effort. Black and Wiliam (1998a) assert, "…self-assessment by the students is not an interesting option or luxury; it has to be seen as essential" (p. 55). The student is the one who must take action to "close" the gap between what they know and what is expected (Sadler, 1989). A teacher can facilitate this process by providing opportunities for participation and multiple points of entry, but students actually have to take the necessary action.

In the opening vignette, students in Ms. K's class are drawing on a range of data sources, including their own and classmates' projects, library research, and interviews with local experts. In preparation for presentations, the students are encouraged to make the connection of the small-scale study they do with plant fertilizer to the larger local system. Opportunities for revisions and regular discussions of what is good work help to clarify criteria as well as strengthen connections and analysis, thus improving learning. Class discussions around

journal reflections provide important data for teachers about student learning and also allow students to hear connections others have made.

For this transition to occur, peer- and self-assessment must be integrated into the student's ways of thinking. Such a shift in the concept of assessment cannot simply be imposed, any more than any new concept can be understood without the student becoming an active participant in the learning. Reflection is a learned skill. Thus, the teacher faces the task of helping the student relate the desired ability to his or her current ideas about assessing one's self and others and how it can affect learning. How do students now make judgments about their own work and that of others? How accurate are these judgments? How might they be improved? Such discussions are advanced immeasurably through the examination of actual student work— initially perhaps by the examination of the anonymous work of students who are not members of the class.

Involving students in their own and peer assessment also helps teachers share the responsibility of figuring out where each student is in relation to the goals or target and also in developing a useful plan to help students bridge the gap. In addition to helping students learn how to learn, there are pedagogical payoffs when students begin to improve their ability to peer- and self-assess. Collecting and utilizing student data for every student in the classroom is made much easier with a classroom of people assisting in the same task. With a clearer vision of peer- and self-assessment and adequate time, teachers can get this help from their students and in the process help them to improve the quality of their own work.

Although there is no one way to develop peer- and self-assessment habits in students, successful methods will involve students in all aspects of the assessment process, not solely the grading after an exercise is completed. If students are expected to effectively participate in the process, they then need to be clear on the target and the criteria for good work, to assess their own efforts in the light of the criteria, and to share responsibility in taking action in the light of feedback. One method that has proved successful has been to ask students to label their work with red, yellow, or green dots. Red symbolizes the student's view that he or she lacks understanding, green that he or she has confidence, and yellow that there appear to be some difficulties and the student is not sure about the quality of the response. These icons convey the same general meaning of traffic lights and are so labeled in the class. This simple method has proved to be surprisingly useful with the colored dots serving to convey at a glance, between student and teacher and between students and their peers, who has problems, where

the main problems lie, which students can help one another, and so on. The traffic-light icons can play another important role, in that they help to make explicit the "big" concepts and ideas of a unit.

With a teacher's help, much useful work in student groups can start from assessment tasks: each member of a group can comment on another's homework, or one another's tests, and then discuss and defend the basis for their decisions. Such discussions inevitably highlight the criteria for quality. The teacher can help to guide the discussions, especially during the times in which students have difficulty helping one another. Peers can discuss strengths and areas of weakness after projects and presentations. Much of the success of peer- and self-assessment hinges on a classroom culture where assessment is viewed as a way to help improve work and where students accept the responsibility for learning—that of their own and of others in their community.

## HOW CAN YOU GET THERE?

Much as Ms. K and Ms. R do in the snapshots of their respective classes, captured in the vignettes, teachers continually make decisions about both the teaching and the learning going on in their classrooms. They make curricular decisions and decide on experiences they think can help further students' understandings.

They decide when and how to introduce and approach a concept and determine an appropriate pace. They continually monitor levels of interest and engagement in curricular activity. They attend to the individual student, the small group, and the class as a whole. If data are collected and used to inform the teacher and student, assessment can play a significant role in all the decisions a teacher makes about what actions to take next. A focus on assessment cuts across multiple standards areas. Box 3-10 shows how teaching standards seek to extend the purview of the teacher.

The teacher is able to see whether students are struggling with an activity or concept, whether they have developed fundamental understandings, whether they need to revisit a particular idea or need more practice to develop particular skills. Teachers need to understand the principles of sound assessment and apply those principles as a matter of daily routine practice.

With the knowledge gained from assessment data, a teacher can make choices. Thus, assessment serves not only as a guide to teaching methods but also to selecting and improving curriculum to better match the interests and needs of the students. According to the Assessment Standards (NRC, 1996), planning curricula is one of the primary uses of assessment data. Teachers can use assessment data to make judgments about

- the developmental appropriateness of the science content,
- student interest in the content,
- the effectiveness of activities in producing the desired learning outcome,
- the effectiveness of the selected examples, and
- the understanding and abilities students must have to benefit from the selected activities and examples. (p. 87)

Thus assessment data can be used immediately, as Ms. K does when she alters upcoming plans, and Ms. R does

---

### BOX 3-10 Assessment in the Teaching Standards

**Teaching Standard C:**

Teachers of science engage in ongoing assessment of their teaching and of student learning. In doing this, teachers

■ use multiple methods and systematically gather data about student understanding and ability;
■ analyze assessment data to guide teaching;
■ guide students in self-assessment;
■ use student data, observations of teaching, and interactions with colleagues to reflect on and improve teaching practice; and
■ use student data, observations of teaching, and interactions with colleagues to report student achievement and opportunities to learn to students, teachers, parents, policy makers, and the general public.

SOURCE: NRC (1996).

when she decides her students are ready to move on to the next stage of activity. The data also are useful when the teachers cover the material again the following year.

## Assessment Should Be Consistent with Pedagogy

For the data to be useful in guiding instructional decisions, the assessment methods should be consistent with the desired pedagogy. Thus, assessment takes into consideration process as well as outcomes and products and the instruction and activities that lead to those ends. Only if assessments in science classrooms can more closely approximate the vision of science education teaching and learning can they inform the teacher's work in trying to implement the emphasis in the *Standards* on students actively doing science.

## Use of Assessment Data

The extent to which any assessment data inform teaching and influence learning depends in a large part on use. Assessment-generated data do little good in the head of the teacher, in the grade book, or by failing to inform future decisions, such as selecting curricula, planning class time or having conversations with students. Teachers must use it to adapt their teaching to meet the needs of their students. In other words, just

as teaching shapes assessment, assessment shapes teaching. The success of formative assessment hinges in large part on how the information is put to use.

With rich assessment data, a teacher can begin to develop possible explanations about what the difficulties might be for the student. If some pedagogical approach did not work the first time, is it likely to be more effective when repeated? Or, is some new approach required? Might other resources be provided? Setting subgoals is another strategy that is often effective. The student is encouraged to take smaller steps toward learning a particular concept or skill.

Peer instruction is another approach that can sometimes work in helping students reach a learning or performance target. If a teacher notices that one student seems to understand (for example, by displaying a green "traffic light") while another does not, the one who understands might help the one who does not. Students occasionally can assist one another because they themselves may have overcome a similar difficulty. Most all teachers use this technique from time to time during class discussion when they encourage the entire group to help a student who clearly is having difficulty. The same principle can operate with just two students working cooperatively when one may have just figured out the desired response and can explain it to the other. Ms. R brought in sixth graders to assist her third graders while they made instruments. Even though help was provided to handle materials and supplies, the older students also could have been more vocal in the design and construction of the instruments.

### Assessment Data Management

Although teachers make assessments all the time, it is important that they develop a system for gathering data about student understanding and progress. This way, no child is overlooked and teachers can be sure that they focus on what they think are the most important learning goals and outcomes. The specific system certainly can vary, depending on a teacher's experience and preferences in gathering such information.

Relying on memory can be difficult with more than 150 students, with many activities, interactions, and observations and over the course of many months before summative evaluations call for the use of such information. One teacher might carry a clipboard while circulating around the room to record comments and observations. Each student has an index card on which to write questions or request an opportunity to speak with the teacher rather than to interrupt. Each day, the teacher observes a handful of students at work but this does not prevent the recording of

information from conversations overheard in the room. This method of collecting data not only helps to organize the teaching but also serves as pertinent information when talking with parents and students. In a review of the relevant research in this area, Fuchs and Fuchs (1986) reported that student achievement gains were significantly larger (twice the effect size) when teachers used a regular and systematic method for recording and interpreting assessment data and providing feedback as compared to when they made spontaneous decisions.

In addition to making good use of the data, keeping good records of day-to-day assessments also is important for summative purposes. When meeting with parents or students, it is helpful to have notes of concrete examples and situations to help convey a point. Good records also can serve to address issues of accountability, a topic that will be discussed in the next chapter.

### THE EQUITY PRINCIPLE

The *Standards* were written with the belief that all students should be expected to strive for and to achieve high standards. According to the *Standards*, in addition to being developmentally appropriate, "assessment tasks must be set in a variety of contexts, be engaging to students with different interests and experiences, and must not assume the perspective or experience of a particular gender, racial or ethnic group" (p. 86). The corresponding principle in classroom assessment is clear: Assessment is equitable and fair, supporting all students in their quest for high standards.

Equity issues are difficult to grapple with and arise at all levels of the education system and in all components of any program. All participants—teachers, students, administrators, curriculum developers, parents—are called upon to share the belief that all students can learn, and this premise needs to infuse all aspects of classroom life. Focusing on equity in classroom assessment is one part of the challenge.

For years, assessment has been used to sort and place students in such a way that all students do not have access to quality science programs (Darling-Hammond, 1994; Oakes, 1985, 1990). Depending on the form assessment takes and how the ensuing data are used, assessment can be a lever for high-quality science education for all rather than an obstacle. In research conducted by White and Frederiksen (1998) where students engaged in peer- and self-assessment strategies, traditionally low-attaining students demonstrated the most notable improvement.

Frequent and immediate feedback to students based on careful attention to daily activity—including student work, observations, participation in conversations and discussions—can provide teachers and students with valuable information. If this information is used in a manner that informs students about standards for improvement and how to attain them, it also can help support all students to achieve their potential.

Assessing students engaged in meaningful activities can promote equity in several other respects as well. For one, teachers can help create a setting where assessment-related activities engage students in experiences that help them synthesize information, integrate experiences, reflect on learning, and make broader connections. Through their regular journal reflections, the students in Ms. K's class reflected on their learning, making connections between their particular project and the local ecosystem. Assessments and assessment-related conversations can help make explicit to all students standards of quality work, make clearer the connections among seemingly unrelated content, concepts, and skills, and provide a scaffold for ongoing student self-assessment (Cole et al., 1999). Misunderstandings of the task or the context, misconceptions about the nature of the task, or difficulties with the language used, can be brought to light and dealt with, often by students helping one another.

Some people believe that the different roles a teacher plays with respect to assessment perpetuates inequitable treatment. In any personal relationship, few of us succeed in treating all of our acquaintances with equal consideration. We may be predisposed by their color, their gender, the way they talk, their social class, whether they respond to us in a warm or in a distant way, and much more. All teachers face such issues as they respond to their students as individuals. Formative assessment requires a close and often personal response. A student's answer to a question may seem strange or not well thought out. Sometimes such reactions may be justified, but sometimes they are prejudgments that may be unfair to the student. In particular, if a student is treated dismissively, then sees another student making a similar response treated with respect, he may be unlikely to try again. So the first and hardest part of treating students equitably is to try to treat all students with the same respect and seriousness. In particular, the idea that everyone has a fixed IQ, that some are bright and some are not, and there is nothing one can do about it, can be very destructive of the kind of interaction necessary between teacher and student to advance learning. If a teacher really thinks in this way, it is highly probable that such an attitude will be conveyed, directly or indirectly, to the student. In the case of one pigeonholed as less "intelligent," the student might believe that this is a true judgment and therefore stop trying.

A different problem that leads to inequity in teaching is associated with problems of "disclosure," the technical label for the challenge of assuring that a student understands the context in which a question is framed and interprets the demand of the question in the way that the teacher intended. Some of these problems are associated with the language of a question or task. For example, both vocabulary and oral style differ among children so the teacher may communicate far more effectively with students from one socioeconomic or ethnic background than with those from another background. Many class questions or homework tasks are set in what are assumed to be realistic settings, often on the assumption that this will be more accessible than one set in abstract. One student's familiar setting, for example, a holiday drive in a car, may be uncommon for another family that cannot afford a car, or even a holiday. Ironically, some research has shown that questions set in "everyday" settings open up wider differences in response between students in advantaged compared with disadvantaged backgrounds than the same questions set in abstract contexts (Cooper & Dunne, 2000).

These problems of "disclosure," and the broader problems of bias in testing have been studied from many aspects in relation to summative tests, especially where these are developed and scored externally from the school. Although such external tests are not subject to the risks of bias at a personal, one-on-one level, this advantage may be offset because a teacher might see that a student does not understand a question and can rephrase to overcome the obstacle, the external grader or machine cannot.

Some people caution against complications associated with the multiple roles that teachers play in assessment, including that of both judge and jury. They see this subjectivity as a threat to the validity of the assessment. They point to a study that examined the effects of expectations on human judgment (Rosenthal & Jacobsen, 1968). Teachers were provided contrived information that a handful of students showed exceptional promise, when in actuality they were no different from the others. When questioned several months later about those students' progress, the teacher reported that they excelled and progressed more than their classmates. One of the basic claims made by the researchers in this study was that the teacher fulfilled the "exceptional-promise" expectation. In efforts to try to overcome or at least abate inherent bias that results in inequitable treatment, teachers, and all those working with students, need to be examined and keep a check on the bias that enters into their own questioning, thinking, and responses.

## VALIDITY AND RELIABILITY

To some, issues of validity and reliability are at the heart of assessment discussions. Although these considerations come into play most often in connection with large-scale assessment activities, technical issues are important to consider for all assessments including those that occur each day in the classroom (American Educational Research Association, American Psychological Association, & National Council on Measurement and Education, 1999). Though principles stay the same, operationally they mean and look different for formative and summative purposes of assessment.

Issues of validity center on whether an assessment is measuring or capturing what is intended for measure or capture. Validity has many dimensions, three of which include content validity, construct validity, and instructional validity. Content validity concerns the degree to which an assessment measures the intended content area. Construct validity refers to the degree to which an assessment measures the intended construct or ability. For example, the *Standards* outline the abilities and understandings necessary to do scientific inquiry. For an assessment to make valid claims about a student's ability to conduct inquiry, the assessment would need to assess the range or abilities and understandings comprised in the construct of inquiry.

Finally, an assessment has instructional validity if the content matches what was actually taught. Questions concerning these different forms of validity need to be addressed independently, although they are often related. Messick (1989) offers another perspective on validity. His definition begins with an examination of the **uses** of an assessment and from there derives the technical requirements. Validity, as he defines it, is "an integrated evaluative judgment of the degree to which empirical evidence and theoretical rationales support the adequacy and *appropriateness of inferences and actions* based on test scores or other modes of assessment" [italics added] (p. 13). Thus, validity in his view is a property of consequences and use rather than of the actual assessment. Messick's (1994) use of validity stresses the importance of weighing social consequences: "Test validity and social values are intertwined and that evaluation of intended and unintended consequences of any testing is integral to the validations of test, interpretation and use" (p. 19). Validity, he argued, needs evidentiary grounding, including evidence of what happens as a result. Moss (1996) urges that actions taken based on interpretation of assessment data and that consequences of those actions be considered as evidence to warrant validity.

Attention to issues of validity is important in the type of ongoing classroom assessment discussed thus far in this chapter. It is important to keep in mind the guideline that says that assessments should match purpose. When gathering data, teachers and students need to consider if the information accurately represents what they wish to summarize, corresponds with subject matter taught, and reflects any unintended social consequences that result from the assessment. Invalid formative assessment can lead to the wrong corrective action, or to neglect action where it is needed. Issues relating to validity are discussed further in Chapter 4.

Reliability refers to generalizability across tasks. Usually, it is a necessary but not complete requirement for validity. Moss (1996) makes a case that reliability is not a necessity for classroom assessment. She argues for the value of classroom teachers' special contextualized knowledge and the integrative interpretations they can make. Research literature acknowledges that over time, in the context of numerous performances, concerns of replicability and generalizability become less of an issue (Linn & Burton, 1994; Messick, 1994). Messick states that dropping reliability as a prerequisite for validity may be "feasible in assessment for instructional improvement occurring frequently throughout the course of teaching or in appraisals of extensive portfolios" (p. 15).

For formative assessments, constraints on reliability are handled differently though still important to consider (Wiliam & Black, 1996). If assessment takes place all the time, a teacher can elicit information that suggests that a previous assessment and judgment was not representative of performance. Teachers are in the position of being able to sample student performance repeatedly over time, thus permitting assessment-based judgments to be adjusted and evolve over a long period of time, leading to confident conclusions.

Teachers, however, must remain open to continually challenging and revising their previously held judgments about student performance. Research suggests that teachers often look for evidence that affirms their own performance (Airasian, 1991) and do not easily modify judgments on individual student achievement (Goldman, 1996; Rosenbaum, 1980).

Although teachers do have a "special-observer" perspective from which they have access to information not generated by way of a test, consideration of technical criteria should remind teachers that careful documentation and systematic observation of all students is necessary to achieve an equitable classroom environment. Assessment data should be "triangulated," or drawn from multiple sources, to reduce the possible bias that may be introduced by any one particular method of obtaining and interpreting evidence.

## Thinking in Terms of the Classroom

Thus far, this chapter has provided a menu of strategies and principles for teachers to consider when designing and implementing a classroom assessment system organized around the goals of improved student work. As noted previously, no one system or collection of strategies will serve all teachers. When choosing among the many available assessment approaches, the following general selection guidelines may be of use. For one, assessments should be aligned with curricular goals, and should be consistent with pedagogy. Because a single piece of work or performance will not capture the complete story of student understanding, assessments should draw from a variety of sources. On a related note, students should be provided with multiple opportunities to demonstrate understanding, performance, or current thinking. Assessments can be most powerful when students are involved in the process, not solely as responders or reactors. Also when designing and selecting assessment, a teacher should consider his or her personal style. Lastly, assessments should be feasible. With large class sizes and competing priorities, some teachers may find it impractical to employ certain practices.

Although any classroom activity can be modified to also serve as an assessment, the data must be fed back into teaching and learning for the assessment to be effective. To the extent that a teacher's decisions and judgments are informed by the information they glean from their students— for example, through observations, class discussions, conversations, written comments, reflections, journals, tests, quizzes, and presentations— teachers can base decisions on understandings of their students and significantly support their learning.

Unfortunately, there are often competing needs and demands on teachers. Teachers have little choice but to juggle the different purposes of assessment in effort to create some coherent system that can best satisfy the different, and often competing, assessment aims. Because they are stretched thin with resources and time, teachers need support in helping them realize the potential of this type of assessment. We turn to this challenge in Chapters 5 and 6.

## KEY POINTS

• To be effective as assessment that improves teaching and learning, the information generated from the activity must be used in such a way as to inform the teacher and/or her students in helping decide what to do next.

• It is important for teachers to have clear performance criteria in mind before they assess student work and responses. These should be conveyed to students.

• Form and content of assessment should be consistent with the intended purpose.

• Student participation becomes a key component of successful assessment strategies at every step. If students are expected to effectively participate in the process, then they need to be clear on the target and the criteria for good work, to assess their own efforts in light of the criteria, and to share responsibility in taking action in light of feedback.

• Assessments should be equitable and fair, supporting all students in their quest for high standards. Thus, technical issues are important to consider for all assessments, including those that occur each day in the classroom.

# 4
# The Relationship Between Formative and Summative Assessment— In the Classroom and Beyond

This chapter discusses the relationships between formative and summative assessments—both in the classroom and externally. In addition to teachers, site- and district-level administrators and decision makers are target audiences. External test developers also may be interested.

Teachers inevitably are responsible for assessment that requires them to report on student progress to people outside their own classrooms. In addition to informing and supporting instruction, assessments communicate information to people at multiple levels within the school system, serve numerous accountability purposes, and provide data for placement decisions. As they juggle these varied purposes, teachers take on different roles. As coach and facilitator, the teacher uses formative assessment to help support and enhance student learning. As judge and jury, the teacher makes summative judgments about a student's achievement at a specific point in time for purposes of placement, grading, accountability, and

informing parents and future teachers about student performance. Often in our current system, all of the purposes and elements of assessment are not mutually supportive, and can even be in conflict. What seems effective for one purpose may not serve, or even be compatible with, another. Review Table 2-1 in Chapter 2.

The previous chapters have focused primarily on the ongoing formative assessment teachers and students engage in on a daily basis to enhance student learning. This chapter briefly examines summative assessment that is usually prescribed by a local, district, or state agency, as it occurs regularly in the classroom and as it occurs in large-scale testing. The chapter specifically looks at the relationship between formative and summative assessment and considers how inherent tensions between the different purposes of assessment may be mitigated.

## HOW CAN SUMMATIVE ASSESSMENT SERVE THE STANDARDS?

The range of understanding and skill called for in the *Standards* acknowledges the complexity of what it means to know, to understand, and to be able to do in science. Science is not solely a collection of facts, nor is it primarily a package of procedural skills. Content understanding includes making connections among various concepts with which scientists work, then using that information in specific context. Scientific problem-solving skills and procedural knowledge require working with ideas, data, and equipment in an environment conducive to investigation and experimentation. Inquiry, a central component of the *Standards*, involves asking questions, planning, designing and conducting experiments, analyzing and interpreting data, and drawing conclusions.

If the *Standards* are to be realized, summative as well as formative assessment must change to encompass these goals. Assessment for a summative purpose (for example, grading, placement, and accountability) should provide students with the opportunity to demonstrate conceptual understanding of the important ideas of science, to use scientific tools and processes, to apply their understanding of these important ideas to solve new problems, and to draw on what they have learned to explain new phenomena, think critically, and make informed decisions (NRC, 1996). The various dimensions of knowing in science will require equally varied assessment strategies, as different types of assessments capture different aspects of learning and achievement (Baxter & Glaser, 1998; Baxter & Shavelson, 1994; Herman, Gearhart, & Baker, 1993; Ruiz-Primo & Shavelson, 1996; Shavelson, Baxter, & Pine, 1991; Shavelson & Ruiz-Primo, 1999).

## FORMS OF SUMMATIVE ASSESSMENT IN THE CLASSROOM

As teachers fulfill their different roles as assessors, tensions between formative and summative purposes of assessment can be significant (Bol and Strange, 1996). However, teachers often are in the position of being able to tailor assessments for both summative and formative purposes.

### Performance Assessments

Any activity undertaken by a student provides an opportunity for an assessment of the student's performance. Performance assessment often implies a more formal assessment of a student as he or she engages in a performance-based activity or task. Students are often provided with apparatus and are expected to design and conduct an investigation and communicate findings during a specified period of time. For example, students may be given the appropriate material and asked to investigate the preferences of sow bugs for light and dark, and dry or damp environments (Shavelson, Baxter, & Pine, 1991). Or, a teacher could observe while students design and conduct water-quality tests on a given sample of water to determine what variables the students measure, and what those variables indicate to them, and how they explain variable interaction. Observations can be complemented by assessing the resultant products, including data sheets, graphs, and analysis. In some cases, computer simulations can replace actual materials and journals in which students include results, interpretations, and conclusions can serve as proxies for observers (Shavelson, Baxter, & Pine, 1991).

By their nature, these types of assessments differ in a variety of ways from the conventional types of assessments. For one, they provide students with opportunities to demonstrate different aspects of scientific knowledge (Baxter & Shavelson, 1994; Baxter, Elder, & Glaser, 1996; Ruiz-Primo & Shavelson, 1996). In the sow bug investigation, for example, students have the opportunity to demonstrate their ability to design and

conduct an experiment (Baxter & Shavelson, 1994). The investigation of water quality highlights procedural knowledge as well as the content knowledge necessary to interpret tests, recognize and explain relationships, and provide analysis. Because of the numerous opportunities to observe students at work and examine their products, performance assessments can be closely aligned with curriculum and pedagogy.

## Portfolios

Duschl and Gitomer (1997) have conducted classroom-based research on portfolios as an assessment tool to document progress and achievement and to contribute to a supportive learning environment. They found that many aspects of the portfolio and the portfolio process provided assessment opportunities that contributed to improved work through feedback, conversations about content and quality, and other assessment-relevant discussions. The collection also can serve to demonstrate progress and inform and support summative evaluations. The researchers document the challenges as well as the successes of building a learning environment around portfolio assessment. They suggest that the relationship between assessment and instruction requires reexamination so that information gathered from student discussions can be used for instructional purposes. For this purpose, a teacher's conception and depth of subject-matter knowledge need to be developed and cultivated so that assessment criteria derive from what is considered important in the scientific field that is being studied, rather than from poorly connected pieces of discrete information.

Researchers at Harvard's Graduate School of Education (Seidel, Walters, Kirby, Olff, Powell, Scripp, & Veenema, 1997) suggest that the following elements be included in any portfolio system:

- collection of student work that demonstrates what students have learned and understand;
- an extended time frame to allow progress and effort to be captured;
- structure or organizing principles to help organize as well as interpret and analyze; and
- student involvement in not only the selection of the materials but also in the reflection and assessment.

An example for the contents for a portfolio of a science project could be as follows:

- the brainstorming notes that lead to the project concept;
- the work plan that the student followed as a result of a time line;
- the student log that records successes and difficulties;
- review of actual research results;
- photograph of finished project; and
- student reflection on the overall project (p. 32).

## Using Traditional Tests Differently

Certain kinds of traditional assessments that are used for summative purposes contain useful information for teachers and students, but these assessments are usually too infrequent, come too late for action, and are too coarse-grained. Some of the activities in these summative assessments provide questions and procedures that might, in a different context, be useful for formative purposes. For example, rescheduling summative assessments can contribute to their usefulness to teachers and students for formative purposes. Tests that are given before the end of a unit can provide both teacher and student with useful information on which to act while there is still opportunity to revisit areas where students were not able to perform well. Opportunities for revisions on tests or any other type of assessment give students another chance to work through, think about, and come to understand an area they did not fully understand or clearly articulate the previous time. In reviewing for a test, or preparing for essay questions, students can begin to make connections between aspects of subject matter that they may not have related previously to one another. Sharing designs before an experiment gets under way during a peer-assessment session gives each student a chance to comment on and to improve his or her own investigation as well as those of their classmates. When performed as a whole class, reviewing helps make explicit to all students the key concepts to be covered.

Selected response and written assessments, homework, and classwork all serve as valuable assessment activities as part of a teacher's repertoire if used appropriately. The form that the assessment takes should coincide with careful consideration of the intended purpose. Again, the use of the data generated by and through the assessment is important so that it feeds back into the teaching and learning.

As shown in Table 4-1, McTighe and Ferrara (1998) provide a useful framework for selecting assessment approaches and methods. The table accents the range of common assessments available to teachers. Although their framework serves all subject-matter areas, the wide variety of

**TABLE 4-1  Framework of Assessment Approaches and Methods**

**HOW MIGHT WE ASSESS STUDENT LEARNING IN THE CLASSROOM?**

| Selected-Response Format | Constructed-Response Format | | | |
|---|---|---|---|---|
| | **Brief Constructed Response** | **Performance-Based Assessment** | | |
| ■ Multiple-choice<br>■ True-false<br>■ Matching<br>■ Enhanced multiple choice | | **Product** | **Performance** | **Process-Focused Assessment** |
| | ■ Fill in the blank<br>■ Word(s)<br>■ Phrase(s)<br>■ Short answer<br>■ Sentence(s)<br>■ Paragraphs<br>■ Label a diagram<br>■ "Show your work"<br>■ Visual representation<br>■ Essay | ■ Research paper<br>■ Story/play<br>■ Poem<br>■ Portfolio<br>■ Art exhibit<br>■ Science project<br>■ Model<br>■ Video/audiotape<br>■ Spreadsheet<br>■ Lab report | ■ Oral presentation<br>■ Dance/movement<br>■ Science lab demonstration<br>■ Athletic skill performance<br>■ Dramatic reading<br>■ Enactment | ■ Debate<br>■ Musical recital<br>■ Keyboarding<br>■ Teach-a-lesson<br>■ Oral questioning<br>■ Observation ("kid watching")<br>■ Interview<br>■ Conference<br>■ Process description<br>■ "Think aloud"<br>■ Learning log |

SOURCE: McTighe and Ferrara (1998).

assessments and assessment-rich activities could be applicable for assessments in a science classroom.

## GRADING AND COMMUNICATING ACHIEVEMENT

One common summative purpose of assessment facing most teachers is the need to communicate information on student progress and achievement to parents, school board officials, members of the community, college admissions officers. In addition to scores from externally mandated tests, teacher-assigned grades traditionally serve this purpose.

A discussion in Chapter 2 defends the use of descriptive, criterion-based feedback as opposed to numerical scoring (8/10) or grades (B). A study cited (Butler, 1987) showed that the students who demonstrated the greatest improvement were the ones who received detailed comments (only) on their returned pieces of work. However, grading and similar practices are the reality for the majority of teachers. How might grading be used to best support student learning?

Though they are the primary currency of our current summative-assessment system, grades typically carry little meaning because they reduce a great deal of information to a single letter. Furthermore, there is often little agreement between the difference between an A and a B, a B

and a C, a D and an F or what is required for a particular letter grade (Loyd & Loyd, 1997).

Grades may symbolize achievement, yet they often incorporate other factors as well, such as work habits, which may or may not be related to level of achievement. They are often used to reward or motivate students to display certain behaviors (Loyd & Loyd, 1997). Without a clear understanding of the basis for the grade, a single letter often will provide little information on how work can be improved. As noted previously, grades will only be as meaningful as the underlying criteria and the quality of assessment that produced them.

A single-letter grade or the score on an end-of-unit test does not make student progress explicit, nor does either provide students and teachers with information that might further their understandings or inform their learning. A "C" on a project or on a report card indicates that a student did not do exemplary work, but beyond that, there is plenty of room for interpretation and ambiguity. Did the student show thorough content understanding but fall short in presentation? Did the student not convey clear ideas? Or did the student not provide adequate explanation of why a particular phenomenon occurred? Without any information about these other dimensions, a single-letter grade does not provide specific guidance about how work can be improved.

Surrounded by ambiguity, a letter grade without discussion and an understanding of what it constitutes does little to provide useful information to the student, or even give an indication of the level of performance. Thus, when a teacher establishes criteria for individual assessments and makes them explicit to students, they also need to do so for grading criteria. The criteria also should be clear to those who face interpreting them, such as parents and future teachers, and incorporate priorities and goals important to science as a school subject area.

Careful documentation can allow formative assessments to be used for summative purposes. The manner in which summative assessments are reported helps determine whether they can be easily translated for formative purposes—especially by the student, teacher, and parents. In the vignette in Chapter 3, a middle school science teacher confers with students as they engage in an ongoing investigation. She keeps written notes of these exchanges as well as from the observations she makes of the students at work. When it is time for this teacher to assign student grades for the project, she can refer to these notes to provide concrete examples as evidence. Using ongoing assessments to inform summative evaluations is particularly important for inquiry-based work, which cannot be captured in most one-time tests. Many teachers give students the opportunity to make

test corrections or provide other means for students to demonstrate that they understand material previously not mastered. Documenting these types of changes over time will show progress and can be used as evidence of understanding for summative purposes.

Teachers face the challenge of overcoming the common obstacle of assigning classroom grades and points in such a way that they drive classroom activity to the detriment of other, often more informative and useful, types of assessment that foster standards-based goals. Grading practices can be modified, however, so that they adhere to acceptable standards for summative assessments and at the same time convey important information that can be used to improve work in a way that is relatively easy to read and understand. Mark Wilson and colleagues at the University of California, Berkeley, have devised one such plan for the assessment system designed for the SEPUP (Science Education for Public Understanding Program) middle school science curriculum (Wilson & Sloane, 1999; Roberts, Wilson, & Draney, 1997; Wilson & Draney, 1997).

The SEPUP assessment system serves as an example of possible alternatives to the traditional, current single-letter grade scheme. As shown in Table 4-2, the SEPUP assessment blueprint indicates that a single assessment will not capture all of the

## TABLE 4-2  SEPUP Assessment Blueprint

### Part 1: Water Usage and Safety

| | | Designing and Conducting Investigations<br>• Designing Investigation<br>• Selecting and Recording Procedures<br>• Organizing Data<br>• Analyzing and Interpreting Data | Evidence and Tradeoffs<br>• Using Evidence<br>• Using Evidence to Make Tradeoffs |
|---|---|---|---|
| 1 | Drinking-Water Quality | | |
| 2 | Exploring Sensory Thresholds | | |
| 3 | Concentration | | |
| 4 | Mapping Death | | |
| 5 | John Snow | | **A:** Using Evidence (p. 52) |
| 6 | Contaminated Water | √: Designing Investigation (p. 61) | |
| 7 | Chlorination | **A:** All elements (p. 66) | |
| 8 | Chicken Little, Chicken Big | | |
| 9 | Lethal Toxicity | √: Organizing Data (p. 94) | |
| 10 | Risk Comparison | √: Analyzing and Interpreting Data (p. 109) | |
| 11 | Injection Problem | | √: Both elements (p. 120) |
| 12 | Peru Story | **A:** Organizing Data **and** Analyzing and Interpreting Data (p. 130) | **A:** Both elements (p. 132) |

SOURCE: Science Education for Public Understanding Program (1995).

Teacher's Guide

**TABLE 4-2  Continued**

## Sections A and B

| | Understanding Concepts<br>• Recognizing Relevant Content<br>• Applying Relevant Content | Communicating Scientific Information<br>• Organization<br>• Technical Aspects | Group Interaction<br>• Time Management<br>• Role Performance/ Participation<br>• Shared Opportunity |
|---|---|---|---|
| 1 | | | |
| 2 | √: Both elements (p. 16)<br>*Measurement and Scale*★ | | |
| 3 | √: Applying Relevant Content (p. 28)<br>*Measurement and Scale*★ | | |
| 4 | | | √: Time Management;<br>Shared Opportunity (p. 38) |
| 5 | | A: Both elements (p.52) | |
| 6 | | | |
| 7 | | | |
| 8 | | | √: Shared Opportunity (p. 76) |
| 9 | A: Applying Relevant Content (p. 97)<br>*Measurement and Scale*★ | | |
| 10 | √: Applying Relevant Content (p. 111)<br>*Measurement and Scale*★ | | |
| 11 | | | |
| 12 | | A: Both elements (p.132) | |

★*Indicates content concepts assessed*

SOURCE: Science Education for Public Understanding Program (1995).

Teacher's Guide

skills and content desired in any particular curricular unit. However, teachers do not need to be concerned about getting all the assessment information they need at a single time with any single assessment.

By using the same scale for the entire unit, the SEPUP assessment system allows teachers to obtain evidence about the students' progress. Without the context or criteria that the SEPUP scoring guide (Table 4-3)

provides, a score of "2" on an assessment, could be interpreted as inadequate, even if the scale is 0-4. However, as the scoring guide indicates, in this example, a "2" represents a worthwhile step on the road to earning a score of "4". In practice, the specific areas that need additional attention are conveyed in the scoring guide, thus a student could receive a "2" as feedback and know what they need to do to improve the piece of

## TABLE 4-3 SEPUP Scoring Guide

### Scoring Guide: Evidence and Tradeoffs (ET) Variable

| Score | Using Evidence<br><br>Response uses objective reason(s) based on relevant evidence to argue for or against a choice. | Using Evidence to Make Tradeoffs<br><br>Response recognizes multiple perspectives of issue and explains each perspective using objective reasons, supported by evidence, in order to make a choice. |
|---|---|---|
| 4 | Response accomplishes level 3, AND goes beyond in some significant way, e.g. questioning or justifying the source, validity, and/or quantity of the evidence. | Accomplishes Level 3 AND goes beyond in some significant way, e.g., suggesting additional evidence beyond the activity that would influence choices in specific ways, OR questioning the source, validity, and/or quantity of the evidence and explaining how it influences choice. |
| 3 | Provides major objective reasons AND supports each with relevant and accurate evidence. | Uses relevant and accurate evidence to weigh the advantages and disadvantages of multiple option, and makes a choice supported by the evidence. |
| 2 | Provides some objective reasons AND some supporting evidence, BUT at least one reason is missing and/or part of the evidence is incomplete. | States at least two options AND provides some objective reasons using some relevant evidence BUT reasons or choices are incomplete and/or part of the evidence is missing; OR only one complete and accurate perspective has been provided. |
| 1 | Provides only subjective reasons (opinions) for choice; uses unsupported statements; OR uses inaccurate or irrelevant evidence from the activity. | States at least one perspective BUT only provides subjective reasons and/or uses inaccurate or irrelevant evidence. |
| 0 | Missing; illegible, or offers no reasons AND no evidence to support choice made. | Missing, illegible, or completely lacks reasons and evidence. |
| X | Student had no opportunity to respond. | |

SOURCE: Science Education for Public Understanding Program (1995).

work. The scoring guide also can provide summative assessments at any given point.

The SEPUP assessment system provides one such example, but teachers can employ other forms of assessment that capture progress as well as achievement at a specific point in time. Keyed to standards and goals, such systems can be strong on meaning for teachers and students and still convey information to different levels of the system in a relatively straightforward and plausible manner that is readily understood. Teachers can use the standards or goals to help guide their own classroom assessments and observations and also to help them support work or learning in a particular area where sufficient achievement has not been met.

Devising a criterion-based scale to record progress and make summative judgments poses difficulties of its own. The levels of specificity involved in subdividing a domain to assure that the separate elements together represent the whole is a crucial and demanding task (Wiliam, 1996). This becomes an issue whether considering performance assessments or ongoing assessment data and needs to be articulated in advance of when students engage in activities (Quellmalz, 1991; Gipps, 1994).

Specific guidelines for the construction and selection of test items are not offered in this document. Test design and selection are certainly important aspects of a teacher's assessment responsibility and can be informed by the guidelines and discussions presented in this document (see also Chapter 3). Item-writing recommendations and other test specifications are topics of a substantial body of existing literature (for practitioner-relevant discussions, see Airasian, 1991; Cangelosi, 1990; Cunningham, 1997; Doran, Chan, and Tamir, 1998; Gallagher, 1998; Gronlund, 1998; Stiggins, 2001). Appropriate design, selection, interpretation and use of tests and assessment data were emphasized in the joint effort of the American Federation of Teachers (AFT), the National Council on Measurement in Education (NCME), and the National Education Association (NEA) to specify pedagogical skills necessary for effective assessment (AFT, NCME, & NEA, 1990).

## VALIDITY AND RELIABILITY IN SUMMATIVE ASSESSMENTS

Regardless of what form a summative assessment takes or when it occurs, teachers need to keep in mind validity and reliability, two important technical elements of both classroom-level assessments and external or large-scale assessments (AERA, APA, & NCME, 1999). These concepts also are discussed in Chapter 3.

Validity and reliability are judged using different criteria, although the two are related. Validity has different dimensions, including content (does the assessment measure the intended content area?), construct (does the assessment measure the intended construct or ability?) and instructional (was the material on the assessment taught?). It is important to consider the uses of assessment and the appropriateness of resulting inferences and actions as well (Messick, 1989). Reliability has to do with generalizing across tasks (is this a generalizable measure of student performance?) and can involve variability in performance across tasks, between settings, as well as in the consistency of scoring or grading.

What these terms mean operationally varies slightly for the kinds of assessments that occur each day in the classroom and in the form of externally designed exams. For example, the ongoing classroom assessment that relies on immediate feedback provides different types of opportunities for follow-up when compared to a typical testing situation where follow-up questioning for clarification or to ensure proper interpretation on the part of the respondent usually is not possible (Wiliam & Black, 1996). The dynamic nature of day-to-day teaching affords teachers with opportunities to make numerous assessments, take relevant action, and to amend decisions and evaluations if necessary and with time. Wiliam and Black (1996) write, "the fluid action of the classroom, where rapid feedback is important,

optimum validity depends upon the self-correcting nature of the consequent action" (pp. 539-540).

With a single-test score, especially from a test administered at the end of the school year, a teacher does not have the opportunity to follow a response with another question, either to determine if the previous question had been misinterpreted or to probe misunderstandings for diagnostic reasons. With a standardized test, where on-the-spot interpretation of the student's response by the teacher and follow-up action is impossible, the context in which responses are developed is ignored. Measures of validity are decontextualized, depending almost entirely on the collection and nature of the actual test items. More important, all users of assessment data (teachers, administrators and policy makers) need to be aware of what claims they make about a student's understanding and the consequential action based on any one assessment.

Relying on a variety of assessments, in both form and what is being assessed, will go a long way to ensuring validity. Much of what is called for in the standards, such as inquiry, cannot be assessed in many of the multiple-choice, short-answer, or even two-hour performance assessments that are currently employed. Reliability, though more straightforward, may be more difficult to ensure than validity. On external tests, even when scorers are carefully calibrated (or done by a machine), variations in a student's performance from day to day, or from question to question, poses threats to reliability.

Viable systems that command the same confidence as the current summative system but are free of many of the inherent conflicts and contradictions are necessary to make decisions psychometrically sound. The confidence that any assessment can demand will depend, in large part, on both reliability and validity (Baron, 1991; Black, 1997). As Box 4-1 indicates, there are some basic questions to be asked of both teacher-made and published assessments. Teachers need to consider the technical aspect of the summative assessments they use in the classroom. They also should look for evidence that disproves earlier judgments and make necessary accommodations. Likewise, they should be looking for further assessment data that could help them to support their students' learning.

## LARGE-SCALE, EXTERNAL ASSESSMENT—THE CURRENT SYSTEM AND NEED FOR REFORM

Large-scale assessments at the district, state and national levels are conducted for different purposes: to formulate policy, monitor the effects of policies and enforce them, make

---

### BOX 4-1 Applying Validity and Reliability Concerns to Classroom Teaching

■ What am I interested in measuring? Does this assessment capture that?

■ Have the students experienced this material as part of their curriculum?

■ What can I say about a student's understandings based on the information generated from the assessment? Are those claims legitimate?

■ Are the consequences and actions that result from this performance justifiable?

■ Am I making assumptions or inferences about other knowledge, skills or abilities that this assessment did *not* directly assess?

■ Are there aspects of this assessment *not* relevant to what I am interested in assessing that may be influencing performance?

■ Have I graded consistently?

■ What could be unintended consequences associated with this assessment?

---

comparisons, monitor progress towards goals, evaluate programs, and for accountability purposes (NRC, 1996). As a key element in the success of education-improvement systems, accountability has become one of the most important issues in educational policy today (NRC, 1999b). Accountability is a means by which policy makers at the state and district levels—and parents and taxpayers—monitor the performance of students and schools.

Most states use external assessments for accountability purposes (Bernauer & Cress, 1997). These standardized, externally designed tests are either norm-referenced tests (NRTs), criterion-referenced tests (CRTs), or some combination of the two. A "standardized" test is one that is to be carried out in the same way for all individuals tested, scored in the same way, and scores interpreted in the same way (Gipps, 1994). NRTs are developed by test publishers to measure student performance against the norm. Results from these tests describe what students can do relative to other students and are used for comparing groups of students. The norm is a rank, the 50th percentile. For national tests, the norm is constructed by testing students all over the country. (It also is the score that test-makers call "at grade level" [Bracey, 1998]). On a norm-referenced test, half of all students in the norm sample will score at or above the 50th percentile, or above grade level, and half will score below the 50th percentile, or below grade level. These tests compare students to other students, rather than measuring student mastery of content standards or curricular objectives (Burger, 1998).

Increasingly, states and districts are moving towards criterion-referenced tests (CRTs), usually developed by state departments of education and districts, which compare student performance to a set of established criteria (for example, district, state or national standards) rather than comparing them to the performance of other students. CRT's allow all students who have acquired skills and knowledge to receive high scores (Burger, 1998).

A well-designed and appropriately used standardized test can generate data that can be used to inform different parts of the system and to assess a range of understandings and skills. Currently, they generally concentrate on the knowledge most amenable to scoring in multiple-choice and short-answer formats. These formats most easily capture factual knowledge (Shavelson & Ruiz-Primo, 1999) and are the most inexpensive in terms of resources necessary for test development, administration, and scoring (Hardy, 1995). Although many of the current standardized tests are intended to assess student achievement, too often they are used only to stimulate competition among students, teachers or schools, or to make other judgments that are not justified by student scores on such tests.

The lack of coherence among the different levels of assessment within the system, often leaves teachers, schools and districts torn between mandated external testing policies and practices, and the responsibilities of teachers to use assessment in the service of learning. These large-scale tests, which often command greater esteem than classroom assessments, create a tension for formative and summative assessment and a challenge for exemplary classroom practice (Black, 1997; Frederiksen, 1984; Smith & Rottenberg, 1991). Teachers are left facing serious dilemmas.

## BUILDING AN EXTERNAL STANDARDS-BASED SUMMATIVE ASSESSMENT SYSTEM

The foundations for a standards-based summative assessment system are assessments that are systemically valid: aligned to the recommendations of the national standards, grounded in the educational system, and congruent with the educational goals for students. Alignment of assessment to curriculum and standards ensures that the assessments match the learning goals embodied in the standards and enables the students, parents, teachers and the public to determine student progress toward the standards (NRC, 1999b).

Assessment and accountability systems cannot be isolated from their purpose: to improve the quality of instruction and ultimately the learning of students (NRC, 1999b). They also must be well understood by the interested parties and based on standards acceptable to all (Stecher & Herman, 1997).

An effective system will provide students with the opportunity to demonstrate their understanding and skills in a variety of ways and formats. The form the assessment takes must follow its purpose. Multiple-choice

tests are easy to grade and can quickly assess some forms of science-content knowledge. Other areas may be better tapped through open-ended questions or performance-based assessments, where students demonstrate their abilities and understandings such as with an actual hands-on investigation (Shavelson & Ruiz-Primo, 1999). Assessing inquiry skills may require extended investigations and can be documented through portfolios of work as it unfolds.

Educators need to be cautious, deliberate, and aware of the strong influence of high-stakes, external tests on classroom practice specific to the instruction emphasis and its assessment (Frederiksen, 1984; Gifford & O'Connor, 1992; Goodlad, 1984; Popham, 1992; Resnick & Resnick, 1991; Rothman, 1995; Shepard, 1995; Smith et al., 1992; Wolf et al., 1991) when considering, implementing, and evaluating large-scale assessment systems. No assessment form is immune from negative influences. Messick (1994) concludes

> It is not just that some aspects of multiple-choice testing may have adverse consequences for teaching and learning, but that some aspects of all testing, even performance testing, may have adverse as well as beneficial educational consequences. And if both positive and negative aspects, whether intended or unintended, are not meaningfully addressed in the validation process, then the concept of validity loses its force as a social value. (p. 22)

Even well-designed assessments will need to be augmented by other assessments. Most criterion-referenced tests are multiple-choice or short-answer tests. Although they may align closely to a standards-based system, other assessment components, such as performance measures, where students demonstrate their understanding by doing something educationally desirable, also are necessary to measure standards-based outcomes. A long-term inquiry that constitutes a genuine scientific investigation, for example, cannot be captured in a single test or even in a performance assessment allotted for a single class period.

## LEARNING FROM CURRENT REFORM

### Beyond a Single Test

Several states and districts are making strides in expanding external testing beyond traditional notions of testing to include more teacher involvement and to better align classroom and external summative assessments, so to better support teaching and learning. The state of Vermont (VT) was one pioneer. The state sought to develop an assessment system that served accountability purposes as well as generated data that would inform instruction and improve individual achievement (Mills, 1996). The system had three components: Students and teachers gathered work for portfolios,

teachers submitted a "best piece" sample for each student, and students took a standardized test. Scoring rubrics and exemplars were used by groups of teachers around the state to score the portfolios and student work samples. Despite the different pieces in place (which also included professional development) the VT experiment faced mixed results and is still evolving. The scoring of the portfolios and student work samples lacked an adequate reliability (in the technical sense) to be used for accountability purposes (Koretz, Stecher, Klein, & McCaffrey, 1994). Many teachers saw a positive impact on student learning, due in part to the focus and feedback on specific pieces of student work that teachers provided to students during the collection and preparation process (Asp, 1998) but also acknowledged the additional time needed for portfolio preparation (Koretz, Stecher, Klein, McCaffrey, & Deibert, 1993).

Kentucky (KY) is another state that made changes to their system and faced similar challenges. The portfolio and performance-based assessment system in that state also did not achieve consistently reliable scores (Hambleton et al., 1995). Both states demonstrate that consistency across scores for samples of work requires training and time. Research on performance assessments in large-scale systems shows that variability in student performance across tasks also can be significant (Baron, 1991).

## Involving Teachers

Teachers who are privy to student discussions and able to making ongoing observations are in the best position to assess many of the educational goals including areas such as inquiry. Therefore, teachers need to become more involved in summative assessments for purposes beyond reporting on student progress and achievement to others in the system. Practices within the United States and in other countries provide us with possibilities of how to better tap into teachers' summative assessments to augment or complement external exams.

In Queensland, Australia, for example, the state moved away from their state-wide examination and placed the certification of students in the hands of teachers (Butler, 1995). Teachers meet in regional groups to exchange results and assessment methods with colleagues. They justify their assessments and deliberate with colleagues from other schools to help ensure that the different schools are holding their students to comparable standards and levels of achievement. Additional examples of the role of teacher judgment in external assessment in other countries are discussed in the next chapter.

Accountability efforts that exclude teachers from assessing their students' work are often justified on grounds that teachers could undermine the reliability by injecting undue subjectivity and personal bias. This argument has some support based on results of efforts in VT and KY. However, as the teachers in Queensland engage in deliberation and discussion (a procedure called **moderation**), steps are taken that mitigate the possible loss of reliability. To help ensure consistency among different teachers in moderation sessions, teachers exchange samples of student work and discuss their respective assessments of the work. These deliberations, in which the standards for judging quality work are discussed, have proved effective in developing consistency in scoring by the teachers. Moderation also serves as an effective form of professional development because teachers sharpen their perspectives about the quality of student work that might be expected, as is illustrated in the next chapter. In the United States, teacher-scoring committees for Advanced Placement exams follow this model.

Moderation is expensive and not always practical. There are other ways to maintain reliability and involve teachers in summative assessments that serve accountability and reporting purposes. In Connecticut, the science portion of the state assessment system involves teachers selecting from a list of tasks and using them in conjunction with their own curriculum and contexts. The state provides the teachers with exemplars and criteria, and the teachers are responsible for scoring their own student work. Teachers can use the criteria in other areas of their curriculum throughout the year.

Douglas County Schools in Colorado rely heavily on teacher judgments for accountability purposes (Asp, 1998). Teachers collect a variety of evidence of student progress towards district standards. Teacher-developed materials that include samples of work, evaluation criteria, and possible assessment tasks guide them. The county uses these judgments to communicate to parents and district-level monitors and decision makers.

Examples and research can help inform large-scale assessment models so that systems produce useful data that inform the necessary purposes while not creating obstacles for quality teaching and learning. Policy and decision makers must look to and learn from reforms underway. After examining large scale testing practices, Asp (1998) offers keys to building compatibility between classroom and large-scale summative assessment systems. His recommendations include the following:

- make large-scale assessment more accessible to classroom teachers;
- embed large-scale assessment in the instructional program of the classroom in a meaningful way; and
- use multiple measures at several levels within the system to assess individual student achievement (pp. 41-42).

When data on individual achievement is not the desired aim (as is often the case when accountability concerns focus on an aggregate level, such as the school, district or region), the use of sampling procedures to test fewer students and to test less frequently can be options.

The assessment systems and features discussed above are not flawless, yet there is much to learn from the experiences of these reforms. Current strategies and systems need to be modified without compromising the goal of a more aligned system. Changes of any kind will require support from the system and resources for designing and evaluating options, informing and training teachers and administrators, and educating the public

## KEY POINTS

- Tensions between formative and summative assessment do exist, but there are ways in which these tensions can be reduced. Some productive steps for reducing tensions include relying on a variety of assessment forms and measures and considering the purposes for the assessment and the subsequent form the assessment and its reporting takes.
- Test results should be used appropriately, not to make other judgments that are not justified by student scores on such tests.

• A testing program should include criterion-referenced exams and reflect the quality and depth of curriculum advocated by the standards.

• For accountability purposes, external testing should not be designed in such a way as to be detrimental to learning, such as by limiting curricular and teaching activities.

• A teacher's position in the classroom provides opportunities to gain useful information for use in both formative and summative assessments. These teacher assessments need to be developed and tapped to best utilize the information that only teachers possess to augment even the best designed paper-and-pencil or performance-based test.

• System-level changes are needed to reduce tensions between formative and summative assessments.

# 5
# Professional Development

Teachers, teacher educators, professional-development specialists, and administrators may be most interested in this chapter.

Improvement by teachers of formative assessment practices will usually involve a significant change in the way they plan and carry out their teaching, so that attempts to force adoption of the same simple recipe by all teachers will not be effective. Success will depend on how each can work out his or her own way of implementing change. (Black, 1997)

Just as there is powerful evidence that formative assessment can improve students' learning and achievement, it is just as clear that sustained professional development for teachers is required if they are to improve this aspect of their teaching. Clear goals are necessary, along with well-understood criteria for high-quality student work. To accurately gauge student understanding requires that teachers engage in questioning and listen carefully to student responses. It means focusing the students' own questions. It means figuring out what students comprehend by listening to them during their discussions about science. They need to carefully consider written work and what they observe while students engage in projects and investigations. The teacher strives to fathom what the student is saying and what is implied about the student's knowledge in his or her statements, questions, work and actions. Teachers need to listen in a way that goes well beyond an immediate right or wrong judgment.

Once the current level of understanding is ascertained, teachers need to use data drawn from conversations, observations, and prior student work to make informed decisions about how to help a student move toward the desired goals. They also need to facilitate and cultivate peer and self-assessment strategies among their students. Although this list is not complete, it does begin to show the scope of professional development that is required to achieve high-quality classroom assessment. Many teachers already engage smoothly and effectively in the processes associated with effective classroom assessment, but these practices need to be developed and enhanced in all classrooms and among all teachers.

## FEATURES OF PROFESSIONAL DEVELOPMENT

Change in assessment practices that are closely linked to everyday teaching will not come about through occasional in-service days or special workshops. Teacher professional-development research (Loucks-Horsley, Hewson, Love, & Stiles, 1998) indicates that a "one-shot" teacher professional-development experience is not effective in almost any significant attempt to improve teaching practice. Because the kind of assessment discussed in this document is intimately associated with a teacher's fundamental approach to her responsibilities and not simply an add-on to current practice, professional development must permit the examination of basic questions about what it means to be a teacher. Professional development needs to become a continuous process (see Professional Develop-

ment Standards, NRC, 1996), where teachers have opportunities to engage in professional growth throughout their careers.

### Rooted in Practice

As Black's statement at the outset of this chapter suggests, widespread formative assessment will not come about solely through changes in policies nor solely by adopting specific programs. New techniques can help, but understanding the basis for the new techniques also is necessary if it is to be implemented in a manner consistent with its intent. Yet a teacher cannot successfully implement all of the changes overnight. Successful and lasting change takes time and deep examination. It becomes critical to root professional-development experiences in what teachers actually do. This approach also is consistent with what research says about teacher learning. A recent study by the NRC (1999a) asserts that teachers continue to learn about teaching in many ways. Primarily, the study states, "they learn from their own practice" (p. 179). Teachers develop repertoires of action that are shaped both by standards and by the knowledge that is gleaned in practice (Wenger, 1998).

### Reflective Practice

The standards for assessment and teaching stress the importance of incorporating reflection into regular teaching practice. The Teaching Standards (NRC, 1996) state that teachers should, "Use student data, observations of teaching, and interactions with colleagues to reflect on and improve teaching practice" (p. 42). Underlying many of the successful professional growth strategies is the use of data from a teacher's own classroom and experience. When teachers examine their own teaching, they begin to notice incidents and patterns that may otherwise have been overlooked. It is important that teachers allow feedback from their own practice to inform their future practice, including their beliefs and understandings involved in teaching. Reflection and inquiry into teaching, and the local and practical knowledge that results, is a start towards improved assessment in the classroom.

One form this inquiry into teaching practice could take is action research, research conducted by teachers for improvement of aspects of their teaching. This form of research is based on the principle that the practical reasoning of teachers is directed toward taking principled action in their own classrooms (Atkin, 1992). By making changes in their own professional activities, teachers learn about themselves and the improvements they desire. Their understanding is deepened when they discuss these experiences with

peers who share similar values and who are trying to make similar changes (Atkin, 1994; Cochran-Smith & Lytle, 1999; Elliot, 1987; Hargreaves, 1998).

## Collaborative

For teachers working in what is often considered a solitary culture, collaboration with peers is thus another feature of improving practices. This is supported by research findings that teachers learn through their interactions with other teachers (NRC, 1999a):

> . . . research evidence indicates that the most successful teacher professional development activities are those that are extended over time and encourage the development of teachers' learning communities. These kinds of activities have been accomplished by creating opportunities for shared experiences and discourse around shared texts and data about student learning, and focus on shared decision making. (p. 192)

Deliberation among peers is a fundamental feature of professional development in any field. These deliberations can be formal or informal and also can occur among colleagues who teach the same grade level or across grades. The exact composition of the group is secondary to the common interest and goal of improved practice. Parallels do exist between what we know about teacher learning and our understanding of student learning. One such parallel is the importance of collecting information that can be used to inform teaching. Collaboration and cooperative groups help facilitate feedback; thus, opportunities that allow colleagues to observe attempts to implement new ideas—by visits to other classrooms and by watching videotape—should be built into professional-development experiences (NRC, 1999a). As well as finding out about effective practices, teachers can glean valuable lessons from sharing and discussing practices that are less than successful (NRC, 1999a). To paraphrase Thomas Edison: I didn't fail; I found out what doesn't work.

## Multiple Entry Points

Because teachers have different professional needs, designers of professional-development programs usually try to provide multiple points of entry to the experience as well as to encourage multiple forms of follow-up. Furthermore, they are cognizant of the fact that change does not happen all at once. To facilitate long-term growth, professional-development experiences need to provide for, and foster as a desired skill, sustained reflection and deliberation.

A major theme throughout this report is that formative assessment practices are, or ought to be, so deeply embedded in instructional practice

that efforts to improve them open up a broad agenda of issues associated with curriculum, instruction, as well as assessment, and the interactions among all three. Figure 5-1 offers a graphic illustration of learning environments. The diagram illustrates that while assessment is a subject for study in and of itself, there will be overlaps with the areas of curriculum (knowledge) and instruction (the students), as well as an inescapable impact on the context in which the learning is taking place. Because of this close integration, examination of classroom assessment is a particularly fertile entry point for the study and

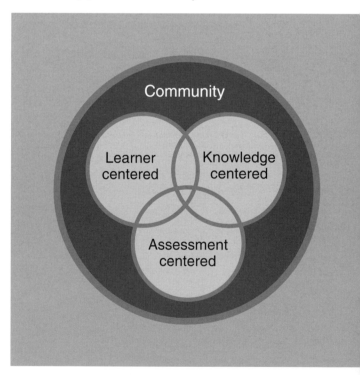

FIGURE 5-1 Perspectives on learning environments.

SOURCE: NRC (1999a).

improvement of a range of teachers' professional activities, all within an integrated context of content, teaching, and learning. It can give impetus and shape to teacher education at all levels, preservice and inservice.

Discussions with groups of teachers focusing on assessment that goes on in their classrooms can quickly lead to some basic questions: What is really worth knowing? What is worth teaching? What counts as knowing? What is competence? What is excellence? How does a particular piece of work reflect what a student understands and is able to do? After conducting classroom assessment professional-development programs with teachers, staff members at TERC (Love, 1999) in Cambridge, Massachusetts, concluded:

> When done well, a discussion by teachers of students' endeavors can lead to deeper understandings about individual students and can provide information about the quality of assignments, teaching strategies and classroom climate. Perhaps most important of all, it provides a rich professional learning opportunity for teachers. (p. 1)

## AN AGENDA FOR ASSESSMENT-CENTERED PROFESSIONAL DEVELOPMENT

This section articulates an agenda necessary to enhance these professional perspectives and to improve these skills. There is no single and clear sequence in which the various issues, skills, and perspectives that are entailed might best be explored and understood in teacher development. A variety of components will be called into play, sooner or later, in any rich program of professional development that starts from a focus on formative assessment. The order in which they arise may well depend on the particular interests and starting points of the teachers involved.

Any comprehensive professional-development program associated with improved formative classroom assessment corresponds closely to the framework for formative assessment itself. That is to say, professional-development activities need to address establishing goals for student learning and performance, identifying a student's understanding, and articulating plans and pathways that help students move towards the set goals. In addition, assessment-centered, professional-development activities need to attend to providing feedback to students, science subject matter, conceptions of learning, and supporting student involvement in assessment.

## Establishing Goals

Clarity about the purposes and goals being pursued in and through the curriculum is essential. Learning how to establish these goals is an important step to improving assessment in one's classroom. In inquiry activities, for example, it is important to keep in mind both the development of the students' understandings and skills about the process of investigation and also the aim of developing concept understanding in relation to the phenomena being studied in that investigation. If skills of communication, or the development to reflect on one's own thinking (metacognition), are aims of the curriculum, then these also have to be in a professional-development agenda.

## Identifying Student Understanding

Implementing effective formative assessment requires that a teacher elicit information about the students' understandings as they approach any particular topic. This is particularly important since a student will likely interpret new material in the framework of her preexisting knowledge and understanding (first main principle from *How People Learn,* NRC, 1999a). Professional development that will lead to improved assessment must begin with the sensitivity to the need of the teacher to learn how to obtain information about a student's current level of understanding of the subject to be taught and learned.

A teacher influenced by the importance of probing student current knowledge started his teaching of a new science topic with questions designed to elicit the existing understanding. He

found that the class knew far more about energy than he had anticipated but lacked a coherent structure in which they could relate their various ideas. He thus abandoned the formal presentations of the whole menu of relevant knowledge that he had emphasized in previous years, and had intended to use again, and attempted instead to help them reorganize their existing understandings. He was able to incorporate student investigations into the unit that helped students' challenge their ideas and apply concepts to everyday events. Overall, the work now took less time than before but was more ambitious in developing understanding of the concepts involved.

As this example demonstrates, teachers must develop and use means to elicit students' existing ideas and understandings. This may be achieved by direct questioning, whether orally, with individuals or in group discussions, or in writing. However, such questioning may be more evocative if it is indirect, if it is about relevant phenomena or situations that are put before students and about which they have to think in order to respond. The responses may then indicate how they interpret the concepts and skills that they possess and choose to bring to bear on the specific problem. For example, the teacher above could ask his students at the outset to try to define mechanical, kinetic or potential energy, or he could provide the students with a scenario, and ask them to discuss the scenario in terms of the types of energy. How best to evaluate and to use the data that come from questioning is equally important to consider and is discussed in a later section.

The analysis here is not simply about a single starting point in a teaching plan.

Curriculum also needs consideration. Content has to be considered in a meaningful way so that subgoals help lead to main goals. Box 5-1 provides an example of subgoals for inquiry science. Teachers may determine the subgoals with different levels of specificity. Some teachers may find dividing a concept

---

### BOX 5-1 Fundamental Abilities and Understandings of Inquiry, 9-12 (Sample)

| Ability | Elaboration |
|---|---|
| Identify questions and concepts that guide scientific investigations. | Students should formulate a testable hypothesis and demonstrate the logical connections between the scientific concepts guiding a hypothesis and the design of an experiment. They should demonstrate appropriate procedures, a knowledge base, and conceptual understanding of scientific investigations. |
| Design and conduct scientific investigations. | Designing and conducting a scientific investigation requires introduction to the major concepts in the area being investigated, proper equipment, safety precautions, assistance with methodological problems, recommendations for use of technologies, clarification of ideas that guide the inquiry, and scientific knowledge obtained from sources other than the actual investigation. The investigation may also require student clarification of the question, method, controls, and variables; student organization and display of data; student revision of methods and explanations; a public presentation of the results with a critical response from peers. Regardless of the scientific investigation performed, students must use evidence, apply logic, and construct an argument for their proposed explanations. |

| Understanding | |
|---|---|
| Scientists usually inquire about how physical, living, or designed systems function. | Conceptual principles and knowledge guide scientific inquiries. Historical and current scientific knowledge influences the design and interpretation of investigations and the evaluations of proposed explanations made by other scientists. |
| Mathematics is essential in scientific inquiry. | Mathematical tools and models guide and improve the posing of questions, gathering data, constructing explanations, and communicating results. |

into too fine a level of detail overly formal. It may deprive them the flexibility of addressing the needs of individual students. Although many of these goals can be determined beforehand, they also may emerge and need to be reevaluated based on assessments occurring during the course of instruction. A check on one step or goal becomes part of the design for the next.

To best help students meet their learning goals, subgoals often have to be identified and articulated. Coming to understand a particular model requires well-organized knowledge of concepts and inquiry procedures, which often requires time and many "little steps" to reach the larger goal. With a solid understanding of science, the underlying structure of the discipline can help serve as the roadmap to guide a teacher in selecting and sequencing activities, assessments, and with their other interactions with students (NRC, 1999a).

*Inquiry and the National Science Education Standards* (NRC, 2000) elaborates on some of the more particular elements of inquiry as ability and understanding for the K-4, 5-8, 9-12 grade spans. Mastering the abilities and understandings associated with inquiry in particular is difficult and can seem elusive even for the most experienced teacher. Such detail would be useful for a teacher when articulating subgoals to support student inquiry in the classroom. Box 5-1 is an example of delineation of the fundamental

abilities and understandings for inquiry at the 9-12 level. For further elaboration, the *Standards* (NRC, 1996) offer complete descriptions of scientific inquiry as abilities and understandings at the K-4, 5-8, and 9-12 levels.

## Articulating a Plan

This process of organizing content into meaningful steps and activities is one of the most demanding aspects of teaching. The teacher needs both a clear idea about the structure of the concepts and skills involved and knowledge of the ways in which students may progress. If intermediary goals are too ambitious, the step towards growth may be too difficult, while if they are too slight, students may not be challenged. An appropriate subgoal is one that goes beyond what the student can learn without help but is within reach given a reasonable degree of teacher support. For more background on the theoretical roots presented here, see Vygotsky's discussion (1962) of the zone of proximal development. Teacher knowledge of common misconceptions and of tools available to promote conceptual reconstruction or to promote fluency with new skills can powerfully inform the process of structuring the curriculum.

## Responding to Students— Feedback

Teachers also need ways to respond to the information they elicit from students. One necessary step is to be able to analyze and interpret students' responses to questions, or their actions in problem situations. In short, teachers need to use data from assessment in order to make appropriate inferences that form the basis of their feedback. This can require careful analysis to probe the meanings behind what students say, write, or do. Questions of good quality are those that evoke evidence relevant to critical points of understanding, but students may often respond in ways that may be hard to interpret. There are many studies that show that seemingly incorrect responses to questions are evidence of a misinterpretation of the question rather than of misunderstanding of the idea being questioned (NRC, 1981). Difficulties with language or in the contexts or purposes of a question are often the cause. Although such difficulties can undermine the validity of formal tests, they need not undermine formative work by the teacher, provided that follow-up questions are used to check, as will happen if question responses are shared and explored in discussion with the teacher or with peers.

### Understanding of Subject Matter

A teacher's interpretation of a student response, questions, and action will be related to that teacher's understanding of the concept or skill that is at issue. Thus a solid understanding of the

subject matter being taught is essential. Performance criteria need to be based on authentic subject matter goals and on a depth of understanding of the subject matter. For formal tests, sound scoring requires careful rubrics—assessment tools that articulate criteria for differentiating between performance levels— that help the assessor to distinguish between the fully correct, the partially correct, and the incorrect response. Such rubrics are even more useful if the variation of common ways in which answers can be partially correct are identified, inasmuch as each partially correct response requires a different kind of help from a teacher in helping a student to progress in overcoming particular obstacles. For an example of a rubric, see Table 4-3 in Chapter 4.

Similarly, less formal assessments also may benefit from a rubric-type tool for interpretation. For example, during a classroom discussion, a teacher can draw on her previous experience with a student's particular difficulty in order to formulate the most helpful oral response.

### Exploring Conceptions of Learning

Underpinning such appropriate rubrics or frameworks will be the teacher's conception of how a student learns both generally and in the particular topic of study. A vision of learning will inform teachers' guidance to students. Addressing issues related to learning may sound formidable but all teachers already have such conceptions, even if they are incomplete and implicit. Ideas about learning are part of any teacher's pedagogic skills; making them explicit so that they can be shared and reflected upon with colleagues may refine these skills.

## SUPPORTING STUDENT INVOLVEMENT IN ASSESSMENT

A central issue for an assessment-centered, professional-development agenda is the development of self-reflection, or metacognition, among students. Evidence of the powers of metacognition can be evoked through a variety of activities: when students are asked to review what they have learned, compose their own test questions, justify to others how their work meets the goals of the learning, and assess the strength and weaknesses of their own work or work of their peers.

Attending to the ways in which students arrived at their results, as well as to the qualities of those results, bears upon and helps give guidance about the metacognitive aspect of students' development. Here, as elsewhere, a clear notion of the meaning and importance of the concept of metacognition has to be developed by the teachers and this notion has to be related to students' work in practice. Reflection and discussion with peers can help begin the examination of these notions.

A focus on student self-reflection raises a final issue. As argued in Chapter 3, an important task required by and promoted by good formative assessment is the cultivation of self-assessment and peer-assessment practices among students. The agenda for the development of the professional capabilities of teachers, or much of it, also can be viewed as an agenda for the development of the capabilities of students to become independent and lifelong learners. In particular, to share with students the goals, as perceived and pursued by their teachers, and to share the criteria of quality by which those teachers guide and assess their work, are essential to their growth as learners. For teachers, this implies a change of understanding of their role, a shift away from being seen as director or controller towards a model of guide or coach.

### An Example

The following vignette highlights many issues previously discussed, offering an example of the sometimes serendipitous nature of assessment-centered professional development. In this case, teachers were working together over the course of a year to design summative assessments and scoring mechanisms and discussing the student work generated during larger scale summative assessment tasks administered at the state level in Delaware.

## Vignette

The task of the Lead Teacher Assessment Committees seemed straightforward: develop end-of-unit assessments for the inquiry-based curricular modules being used in elementary schools across the state. After months of often frustrating efforts, it was not until the teachers recognized that they first needed to examine their values, beliefs, and assumptions about student learning, and, in turn, the design and purpose of the assessments they were being asked to develop, that any substantive progress was made. What emerged from this process was a self-created learning organization in which assessment became a force that would support and inform instructional decision making at multiple levels of Delaware's science education system. Just how this process evolved will be related through the professional-development experiences of a team of fifth-grade teachers charged with the responsibility of creating a performance-based assessment for an ecosystem module.

From the very beginning in 1992, Delaware's standards-based reform initiative included teachers in crucial roles, such as the development of the state science content standards and with the framework commission. Within this 1997 reform context, elementary lead teachers from across the state began to collaborate on the development of end-of-unit performance assessments for the curricular modules used in their classrooms. Even though the teaching guides that accompanied the modules included assessments, many Delaware teachers felt that the majority of the assessment items did not elicit the kinds of responses needed to determine if their students really understood the major concepts central to the State Science Standards. Although the teachers were in agreement that the accompanying assessments were inadequate, there was very little agreement as how to best proceed in developing alternative assessments. After days of discussion, the team of fifth-grade teachers decided to begin by constructing a concept map to ensure that there was consensus about which "big ideas" and processes from the ecosystem module they considered important enough to assess.

What happened next was not only a surprise to the teachers but also to the leaders facilitating the development process. As the concept map began to take shape, it became apparent that many of the teachers were confusing the skills their students needed to perform the ecosystem activities with the major concepts they needed to understand. Attempts to clarify the confusion led to a series of conversations in which the teachers realized that in their zeal to provide "hands-on" experiences, they had often taught scientific processes in isolation from or at times, to the exclusion of, scientific concepts. Consequently, observing the ecocolumn and constructing observation charts had taken precedence over students explaining the relationship between the living and nonliving components of the ecocolumn they were studying.

In efforts to determine the cause of the over-emphasis, the assessment-development team made some interesting discoveries. The teachers began to openly acknowledge that even though each of them had participated in 30 hours of professional development centered on the ecosystem module they still did not feel comfortable with some important ecological concepts. This conversation was especially insightful for the leaders facilitating the development process, since they had assumed that 30 hours of professional development were adequate. At that point in the process, it became clear that once again the time table for developing the assessments needed to be modified for the teachers to better understand the concepts they were being asked to teach and develop an assessment around.

Through this period of self-discovery, the teachers also began to realize as they reviewed the teacher's guide, that their perceptions regarding what should be emphasized during the course of the unit had been strongly influenced by the wording and formatting of the guide. Because the titles of most of the ecosystem activities began with action verbs, such as "observing," "adding," "setting up," they had naturally inferred that their instructional focus should be process oriented. As the team of fifth-grade teachers became more confident about their content knowledge and more comfortable with their newly acquired role of being a "wise curricular consumer," they were able to identify the major concepts from the Delaware Science Standards they did not feel had been made explicit enough in the ecosystem module. They also began to rethink how the investigative activities needed to be presented and taught to support and strengthen students' conceptual understandings. This rethinking automatically led to the kinds of assessment discussions they had been unable to engage in for weeks. With a new and collective understanding about the module's instructional goals, the challenge for the team of teachers became twofold: how to create a performance-based assessment that could be used to evaluate both a student's skill level and conceptual understandings and how not to reinforce the process/concept dichotomy they themselves had experienced.

Several other crucial lessons learned by the assessment-development team were the importance of using educational research to inform decision-making processes and the need to seek outside expertise to stretch the thinking of team members. One of the most challenging issues facing the team was ensuring that the assessment items under development could be used to evaluate a range of student capabilities—from making accurate observations to formulating well-reasoned explanations. They included discussions about how items had to match what they were being asked. For example, if they wanted to assess critical reasoning, they had to probe in areas that would elicit that.

As Figure 5-2 shows, once a draft version of the ecosystem assessment was finally developed, the team began efforts to construct scoring criteria. Initially, attempts were made to develop very generic or holistic scoring rubrics, but the team soon realized that if these assessments were going to be used to inform teachers' instructional practices, generic rubrics were simply not diagnostic enough. The problem then became "so now what?" Leaders facilitating the team efforts once again realized the need to look beyond the expertise of the group for an alternative to generic rubrics so they brought in an assessment expert who was willing to work with the teachers in the process.

Bringing in an outside expert was good for the entire process. In conversations that ensued in the expert's presence, the teachers accepted that all of the students did not get the answers wrong for the same reason. It also was through the expert's insistence that the team began to explicitly state the criteria for a complete response. This exercise would initiate some of the most interesting discussion that occurred during the entire development process. As the debates about the criteria got into full swing, the teachers recognized that, because they each had their own set of internalized criteria for evaluating student work, what was considered quality work in one of their classes was not necessarily considered quality work in another. Having to explicitly state the criteria became the impetus for very intense discussions regarding what counts as evidence of student learning and how good is good enough. These discussions would be revisited again and again and evidence of student learning would ultimately become the foundation for the decision-making assessment process.

Although the plan had always been to pilot draft versions of the ecosystem assessment so that student work could be used to modify both the instrument and scoring criteria, none of the team members anticipated how profoundly many of their assumptions about student learning would be challenged by critically examining and analyzing student work. Because so much time and effort had gone into the design of the assessment instrument and scoring rubrics, team members felt very confident that they had developed a quality product. The teachers naturally experienced a great sense of ownership regarding the assessment and although the process at times had been grueling they felt very proud of their efforts. When samples of student work from the pilot were returned for scoring and analysis and were not the quality anticipated, the first tendency was to blame the students. It took several rounds of discussions and more objective evaluations of student responses before the team was ready to admit that at least some of the problem was the way in which the items or rubrics had been designed. By examining student responses from across the state it was difficult to ignore converging evidence, which strongly suggested that some items were obviously confusing and therefore did not allow students the best opportunity to demonstrate their understandings. Box 5-2 presents two samples of student work to illustrate this point. The samples are typical student responses for the item that appeared on the piloted version, as shown in Figure 5-2.

After samples of earlier versions of the assessment-generated student work had been analyzed, it became apparent that the item itself was contributing to students' oversimplification of an important scientific concept—interdependency of organisms within an ecosystem. In their efforts to reduce the complexity of the wetland assessment item, the lead teachers were inadvertently fostering a very linear model of interdependency and were actually setting the students up to respond incorrectly. The overwhelming state-wide response, if the large-mouth bass disappeared then the heron would automatically die and nothing would happen to other organisms, literally forced the lead teachers to not only take a much closer look at the item but also to begin to question reasons for the prevalence of such a response.

In a revised version in Figure 5-3, the item was rewritten to reinforce a web-like model of interdependency that more closely approximates what actually occurs in the wetland ecosystems. Results from the subsequent field tests indicated that the modifications to the item are in part responsible for more complete and accurate student responses as seen in Box 5-3. In their responses to this item, more students included mention of how populations of organisms would be impacted rather than how a single organism would be affected.

Several other factors contributed to an increase in student performance on this item. As the lead teachers began to focus on acquiring evidence of student understanding, they realized several important things about their instructional practice. For one, most of their instructional emphasis had focused exclusively on the student-built ecocolumns and

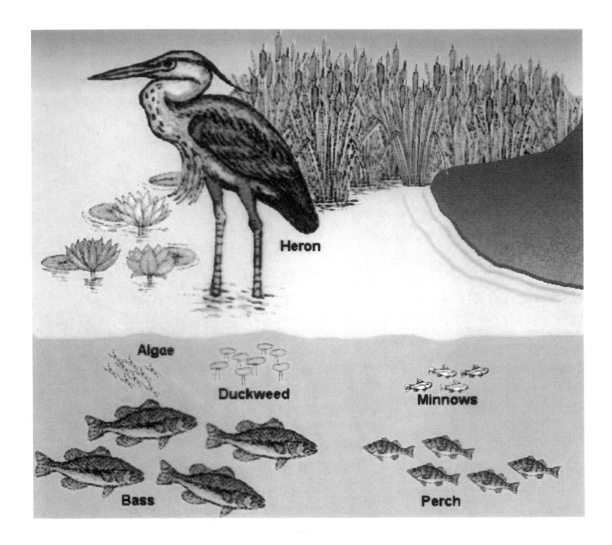

**Wetland Ecosystem**

Look at the picture of the wetland ecosystem. You could find several food chains in this ecosystem. Here is one example.

Algae ⟶ Minnows ⟶ Perch ⟶ Large-Mouth Bass ⟶ Heron

If all the Large-Mouth Bass disappear, explain how the remaining organisms in the ecosystem would be affected.

---

FIGURE 5-2 First version of assessment item.
SOURCE: Adapted from Delaware Science Coalition (1999).

not on creating a learning environment in which students were encouraged and challenged to extend their own understandings beyond their own ecocolumn model to other local ecosystems. The responses to the item have prompted teachers to go beyond the kit to exploring local habitats. Additionally, the conversations revealed that many of the teachers also had developed the linear interdependency model that their student subscribed to in their responses. Clarifying this particular content issue with teachers resulted in immediate and significant improvement in student responses. Teachers continue to work collaboratively to develop assessment items and rubrics aligned with their curriculum and to identify areas that would prove rich for further professional development.

---

**BOX 5-2 Student Work from Original Version**

**Sample #1**

The perches will have a big population since the large mouth bass is gone, and the heron would die since there is no more large mouth bass.

**Sample #2**

The Heron wouldn't have anything to eat because the Heron eats the Bass. The perch wouldn't die because nothing will eat it.

SOURCE: Delaware Science Coalition (1999).

---

As the Delaware experience indicates, groups of teachers and other experts coming together around student work can be a powerful experience. The "messiness" of this professional-development experience is in many ways its very strength. It also demonstrates a realistic view of the complexity of assessment-related discussions. Allowing the valuable conversations to emerge and run their course provided a richness that may not have been captured in a session with a strict agenda. Also, it certainly would not have happened in a single scoring session. The conversations about scoring student work, assessment criteria, or assessment designs quickly get to issues of content and questions of worth.

One important element highlighted in the Delaware experience was the discussion concerning the valid inferences that can be made from assessment data. All teachers must grapple with this issue as they use assessment data to inform teaching decisions. In this instance, asking critical questions such as, "What does this piece of evidence show?" and "What else do I need to find out?" led the teachers to identify the flaws in this experience.

Also conveyed in this case, efforts to use assessment as a cornerstone of teacher-professional development can spawn a deeper knowledge of science content. To design the assessment and score the students' work, teachers had to probe and extend their own under-

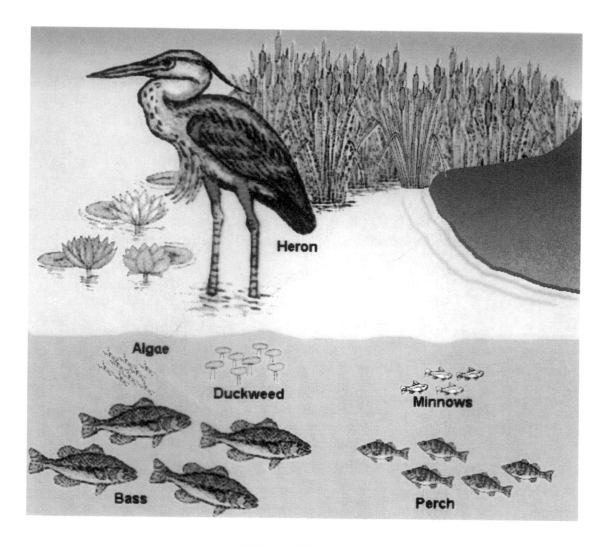

**Wetland Ecosystem**

Look at the picture of the wetland ecosystem. You could find several food chains in this ecosystem. Here is one example.

Sun ⟶ Algae ⟶ Minnows ⟶ Perch ⟶ Large-Mouth Bass ⟶ Heron.

The heron is a bird that can eat many kinds of fish in the wetland. If all the Large-Mouth bass disappear, explain how the interdependency of two of the remaining organisms in the food chain may be affected.

---

FIGURE 5-3   Revised version of assessment item.
SOURCE: Adapted from Delaware Science Coalition (1999).

## BOX 5-3 Student Work from Revised Version

### Sample #1

A lot of perch will be alive so that, means they will eat even more minnows and if theres not much the fish wont be able to eat some of the duckweed and if they don't eat the duckweed there will be to much. There won't be any plants alive because the duckweed will cover the Pond.

### Sample #2

No bass will eat the perch so the perch would grow out of control. Another thing would be that all the perch would eat all the minnows.

SOURCE: Delaware Science Coalition (1999).

standings. Many of the teachers discovered that even they did not fully grasp all of the ecology concepts being taught and assessed. The teachers recognized that they were led by the wording and format of the curriculum guide rather than their own understanding of the material. Identifying and addressing areas where teachers need additional support to better learn the content is very important especially when one considers research showing that a lack of science-content knowledge limits a teacher's ability to give appropriate feedback, including identifying misconceptions (Tobin & Garnett, 1988). In her 1993 work, Deborah Ball demonstrated the importance of subject-matter knowledge in teaching students for understanding, which requires careful listening to why and what the students are saying.

Numerous routes can be taken for professional development aimed at improving assessment and understanding of students. For example, placing student work at the center of their efforts, Project Zero brings teachers together to discuss and reflect on assessment practices and student work. Teachers involved in the project engage in a "collaborative review process" as they look critically and deeply at student work. They are urged to stick to the piece of work and not look for psychological and social factors that could prevent a student from producing strong work (NRC, 1999a).

In a 13-country study of 21 innovations in science, mathematics, and technology education, the researchers noted (Black & Atkin, 1996) seven essential elements of programs that were successful in promoting changes in teachers. These elements are displayed in Box 5-4.

Attention to the assessment that occurs in their classrooms forces teachers to focus on some aspect of their practice. Assessment-centered, professional development regardless of the starting point can be a powerful vehicle for teacher professional growth when performed collaboratively, with regular reflection, and based on knowledge gleaned in practice.

## KEY POINTS

• Professional development becomes a lifelong process directed towards catalyzing professional growth.

• Assessment offers fertile ground for teacher professional development across a range of activities because of the close integration of assessment, curriculum, teaching and learning.

There is no "best" place to start and no "best" way to proceed.

• Professional development should be rooted in real-world practice.

• Regular and sustained reflection and inquiry into teaching is a start towards improved daily assessment.

• Collaboration is necessary, as is support at the school and broader systems level.

---

**BOX 5-4   Some Basic Features of Professional Development**

■ Change begins with disequilibrium—a perception that current practices and policies cannot help the teachers achieve their goals. If that perception does not exist, then any voluntary project will have to create it.

■ Teacher networks can be powerful. Describing the effects of setting up networks, one project reported: "Exposure [to other ideas, resources, and opportunities] broadens teachers' awareness of possibilities for change and fosters a sense that alternatives to traditional knowledge and beliefs, classroom practices, and professional involvement are available and within their reach."

■ Teachers react against ideas and materials that are theoretically sound but do not function in the classroom. They seek proof that other professionals with whom they identify are making new methods work. Such existence proof—the fact that others can do it—gives them moral support and challenges them.

■ Demonstrating an idea to teachers in action in a real context deepens their understanding in powerful, subtle, and manifold ways. Such modeling adds to the existence proof the proof of the teacher's own experience.

■ Innovation is risky. Personal support—which much be both knowledgeable and close at hand—is then essential, as the isolated teacher can easily lose direction and lose heart when the inevitable, often unexpected, difficulties arise.

■ It is most often the case that the whole environment of schools which demonstrably promote effective professional development also encouraged experimentation.

■ We know from research into teachers' professional development that change without reflection is often shallow and incompetent. Such reflection must follow on experimentation, however well or badly an experiment may turn out. Yet teachers are rarely given the time or stimulus for reflection.

SOURCE: Black and Atkin (1996).

# 6
# Beyond the Classroom— System-Level Supports

This chapter speaks to people in decision-making and policy positions at the school, district, state and national levels. Parents and community members also may also be interested in this discussion about the broader system level.

Policies throughout the education system can have a profound influence on classroom practice. At the very least, enhanced assessment in the classroom requires consistent and compatible action from school, district, and state levels. Already stretched thin with the day-to-day teaching responsibilities, teachers need broad-based support and backing when it comes to improved assessment of student learning. Thus, change and support within the system needs to occur at many levels including higher education institutions, and it also must enlist the assistance of parents, other community members, and the public media.

There is no one best way to support teachers in their ongoing assessment and advancement of student learning. Changes should be consistent with, and supportive of, the vision for science education set forth in the *Standards* and the vision for classroom assessment set forth in this document. Change takes time; results cannot be expected overnight. Schools and districts need to provide a sustained focus for improved classroom assessment, rather than have it sit within the ever-shifting list of priorities that often come with changes in political parties and school leadership and administration. Here we will examine provisions that must be made at state, district, school, and community levels to enhance the types of classroom assessment recommended in this document.

## DISTRICT AND STATE TESTING POLICIES

School-testing policies need to be reexamined and revamped to realize the goals for classroom assessment outlined in this volume. In terms of large-scale testing for program monitoring and accountability purposes, the *Standards* stress that "[A]ssessment policies and practices should be aligned with the goals, student expectations and curriculum frameworks" (NRC, 1996, p. 211). Designing quality assessments that assess the full range of science education is particularly important considering the significant impact "high-stakes" testing has on classroom teaching and assessment practice (Darling-Hammond, 1994; Gifford & O'Connor, 1992; Linn, 2000; Oakes, 1985, 1990; Resnick & Resnick, 1991; Smith, Hounshell, Copolo, & Wilkerson, 1992).

Accountability is an important feature of our educational system, but the current models used for implementation of accountability policies are far from sufficient. Useful data often is generated at the expense of detrimental effects on classroom practice and student learning (Darling-Hammond, 1994; Gifford & O'Connor, 1992; Gipps, 1994; Goodlad, 1984; Smith et al., 1992). In particular, high-stakes external assessments often drive curriculum and classroom assessment practices (Frederiksen & Collins, 1989; Haney & Madaus, 1994; Linn, 2000; NRC, 1987).

External assessments should be criterion-referenced and aligned to the recommendations of standards, curriculum, and instruction. Not only will effective assessments match exemplary instructional practices, they also will assess what is important and valued, not solely what is easily and inexpensively measured. In science education, this includes assessing and supporting the development of inquiry as a key component of science education. To support the *Standards'* vision of quality science and to attend to inquiry will require that we reconsider ways in which to involve teachers in the large-scale assessment process.

One alternative solution may be for school districts to establish their own local standards-based accountability system in tandem with those of their state. Ideally, carefully designed tests would allow districts to develop and implement assessments in core curriculum areas, such as science, that match their learning goals, demonstrate student achievement of standards, inform instruction, guide professional development, and demonstrate program impact. Teachers can take a role in the development of these assessments. The assessment development situation in Delaware as described in Chapter 5 offers such an example at the state level. However, what works for a small state like Delaware may not be as feasible for larger states, especially where curricular decisions are made at the district level. With such a system, district and state policy makers and the public may be provided with a picture of student and system performance that is both more valid and more reliable.

## TEACHERS' VOICE IN EXTERNAL SCIENCE ASSESSMENTS

No one has as much information as the teacher does about student accomplishments and abilities. It is recognized that a teacher's daily presence in the classroom affords intimate knowledge of student achievement and learning that is valued highly and impossible to capture on a test. The challenge becomes one of tapping into this knowledge for purposes of reporting about the quality of student learning. We can look to districts, states and other countries that have made reforms in their assessment policies and practices for some examples of possibilities (see Chapter 4), as well as to learn from their successes and challenges.

Efforts to keep teachers from contributing to external assessments are often made on grounds that including them could undermine the assessment's reliability. Teacher deliberation is one possibility to help ensure consistency among different teachers. In moderation sessions, teachers exchange samples of student work and discuss their respective assessments of the work. The result

of these sessions has proved to be effective in terms of developing common criteria for scoring (Wood, 1991). It also is valuable for the teacher's professional development, also noted in Chapter 5. The scoring of Advanced Placement examinations follows this model and serves as an example of how teachers can be more heavily involved in this type of assessment. However, productive sessions require careful planning and intensive preparation so that teachers come to achieve common standards and consistently and reliably use those standards to evaluate student work. In recent years, a Vermont initiative to involve teachers in the external evaluation of student portfolios ran into obstacles with teachers scoring inconsistently across raters, which resulted in differing summative judgments (Stecher & Herman, 1997).

## DISTRICT AND SCHOOL LEVEL

In addition to general testing policies, responsibilities fall to district policy makers and school administrators to create structures that facilitate high-quality, classroom-based assessment. Professional development for teachers (Chapter 5), provisions of time during the school day, resources—both materials and people—are among the many steps necessary to help build the capacity of the system to make use of teacher knowledge to enhance student learning.

## Professional Development

Teachers need opportunities to engage in assessment-related professional development with colleagues where they can reflect on their own teaching practice and that of others and discuss student work (see Chapter 5). Together, through collaboration and reflection, teachers can expand their assessment repertoires and understanding; and in turn, they can better support student learning through improved formative assessment in their own classrooms.

Teachers who acknowledge the importance of assessment, especially the potential of ongoing formative assessments, may feel constrained by numerous issues and tensions. In addition to the pressures levied by the external tests, constraints may include time, class size, resources, training, administrative support, and parental understanding and support.

## Time

In schools and districts implementing standards-based science programs, time is built into the school day and week for teachers to meet and work with their colleagues so that they can engage in meaningful discussions about student work and learning; discuss assessment strategies; and learn how to appropriately use data from student work, observations and other formative assessments to inform

their practice. There also is time structured into the school day and week for teachers to meet and talk with students about their progress both individually as well as in groups and also to observe students as they work. Shared-preparation periods also offer teachers the opportunities for conversations to share reflections and connections about learning, teaching and assessment. Teachers frequently meet with school administration and support personnel to discuss and plan assessment strategies and to learn about current research that supports their ideas.

Unfortunately, this is not the reality experienced by most teachers. Many teachers are caught in a tension between trying to implement a standards-based program and the confines of a traditionally structured day. The fragmentation of their day and the pressures of bells, assigned yard and bus duties, parent meetings, and paper work, particularly for high school teachers, who may have 150 students per day or more, serve to focus their efforts on simply surviving day by day (Aschbacher, 1993). When time is scheduled for teachers to meet, it is usually reserved for short staff meetings scheduled at the end of the day, or folded into inservice days. Current research maintains that one of the key barriers to the implementation of new assessment practices in the classroom by teachers is the lack of time with professional colleagues to discuss, learn, plan, practice, use and reflect (Aschbacher, 1993).

Just as time can influence the content selected for instruction and how it is taught, it also can influence the type, frequency and thoroughness of assessments. Carving out the time to engage in ongoing assessment of all students requires a shift in the conceptual understanding of the teaching process itself. Darling-Hammond and colleagues (1995) conducted case studies of five schools where teachers and students throughout the school were actively engaged in formative assessment. In describing the shifts in instruction that were supportive of improved classroom assessment, Darling-Hammond and her colleagues maintain that teachers moved from the role of instructors to that of facilitators. As facilitators, the teachers created learning opportunities for their students that encouraged students to engage in their own work. This provided teachers with the opportunity to observe students' work, to talk with them about what they were learning, and to use these observations to inform their teaching.

Regular time also needs to be provided during the school day for teachers to take part in professional growth activities, conduct research on their teaching practices, observe other classrooms, use available external resources, and attend professional meetings and conferences (NRC, 1996).

## Class Size

Although several states have recently implemented strategies to reduce the number of students assigned to classrooms at the primary and elementary levels, most middle and high school classrooms are still over-crowded. Additionally, with departmentalized courses in many middle and secondary schools, teachers often find themselves teaching 150 or more students per day. When faced with large numbers of students and other site obligations, teachers may have a difficult time maintaining continuous classroom assessments.

However, because assessment information is such a powerful tool for supporting student understanding and learning, even science teachers with large classes can find ways to incorporate multiple ongoing assessment strategies into their instructional activities. Student self-assessment, for example, is not only an essential tool for developing student self-directed learning, it also can provide a means for teachers with large classes to successfully incorporate ongoing assessment practices into their instruction. Through self-assessment, students are able to reflect on, internalize, and take responsibility for their own learning. With the teacher serving as consultant, students develop scoring rubrics and criteria to judge their own and their peers' work.

When teachers treat students as serious learners and serve as coaches rather than judges, students come to understand and apply standards of good scientific practice (NRC, 1996).

### Administrative Support

For teachers to implement authentic and meaningful assessment activities in the classroom, they need access to resources within the school (materials, equipment, media and technology) and outside of the school (researchers, scientists, other specialists and community members). Teachers also need support from school and district administration, and understanding from parents about new assessment practices. School leaders must structure and sustain suitable support systems for the work that teachers do (NRC, 1996). Strong commitment from district administration to provide support for teachers can have a profound effect on the effectiveness of assessment reform (Aschbacher, 1993).

Teachers not only need administrative support to design and successfully implement ongoing assessments in their classrooms, they also need support from administration in helping parents to understand why their assessment practices might look different. Many parents may want their children to be taught and tested as they were in school—rote memory

and standardized tests—and teachers must be supported and prepared to explain and justify why they are assessing children differently (Aschbacher, 1993).

### HIGHER EDUCATION

Colleges and universities need to make classroom assessment an integral part of their teacher-education programs. Just as classroom teachers can gain tremendously from seeing and discussing exemplary practice, so too can preservice teachers. Currently, only 14 of the 50 U.S. states explicitly require competence in assessment as a condition to be licensed to teach. Only 3 of the 50 states demand competence in assessment to be licensed as a principal. There is not a single certification examination in use in any context or at any level in the United States today that verifies competence in classroom assessment for teachers or administrators (Stiggins, 1999). Therefore, colleges of education, who naturally prepare their graduates for certification in their state, see no need to offer the classroom-assessment training that teachers need to do their jobs. It has been this way for decades. This will not change until policy makers factor an expectation of assessment literacy into teacher and principal qualifications. Improving assessment so that it truly works in the service of learning calls for research to be conducted at all levels—from the classroom to exploring the formative-summative link. University researchers also can serve as a resource for school districts and teachers. In both science content and teaching methods course work, faculty should model appropriate assessment strategies that support and promote learning.

## COMMUNITY AND PARENTS

For a modified assessment system to succeed, all of the players need to be better informed about assessment issues and the desirable features of a contemporary science education program. Without an idea of what a quality science program, including quality assessment, looks like, one grounded in best classroom practice, decision making may not serve the best interests of students and learning. This is true for parents and community members as well as state-level policy makers. Parents need to be educated on the purposes and consequences of assessment practices. Likewise, a forum should be provided for them to voice their questions and concerns, especially in today's climate of increasing reliance on external, standardized tests. Parents will be faced with interpreting test results and perhaps influencing some assessment-relevant decisions, for example, the form for communicating student progress. Because

parents are major consumers of assessment data, all those responsible for providing education to children—teachers, site-level and district-level administrators, and state-level policy makers—must take some of the responsibility for keeping them informed about assessment practices that are most likely to help their children learn.

## TOWARD WHAT END?

The main points of this report to the *National Science Education Standards* (1996) are straightforward. Many of the assessment procedures the teacher employs, particularly those we call formative, can serve directly to enhance the students' learning in ways that are not possible with any other type of assessment tool. However, teachers need time and assistance in developing these procedures.

Furthermore, the student's understanding of a contemporary view of science cannot be assessed for summative purposes without substantive contributions from the student's own classroom teacher. To be complete, assessments that are used to certify what a person knows cannot be adequate without making use of what the teacher uniquely knows about the individual student. Only the teacher can know how a particular student pursues an investigation that may extend over several days or weeks. Only the teacher knows how a student confronts and works through the inevitable challenges that arise. Only the teacher has the opportunity to probe beneath the one-word response to ascertain how deeply a student understands the concepts she is trying to teach.

Still, we must learn how to make teacher judgments trustworthy. Many other countries have reached this stage in their assessment systems, but such an outcome takes sustained work. For one thing, teachers need more time than they are usually afforded to work in collaboration with other teachers to hone their ability and consistency in judging student work (moderation). Furthermore, for the necessary levels of public confidence and trust in the process to develop, the procedures devised and employed when the teachers' role in summative judgments is increased must be made transparent. School administrators and policy makers, as well as teachers themselves, have a responsibility to keep the public informed.

But these goals, even in the ideal, do not lead to elimination of all external tests (standardized or not) or other forms of accountability that are not based as much on teachers' direct knowledge of the student. Rather, a way must be found of combining and maintaining consistency between the results of external tests and those of well-informed and moderated teacher judgments. Above all, the total assessment system must be complementary, with each part supporting the other, with each providing distinctive information, and with all parts aligned with the development of higher standards.

# References

Airasian, P. W. (1991). *Classroom assessment.* New York: McGraw Hill.

American Educational Research Association, American Psychological Association, and National Council on Measurement and Education. (1999). *Standards for educational and psychological testing.* Washington, DC: American Educational Research Association.

American Federation of Teachers, National Council on Measurement in Education, and the National Education Association. (1990). *Standards for teacher competence in educational assessment of students.* Washington, DC: Author.

Ames, C. (1992). Classrooms: Goals, structures, and student motivation. *Journal of Educational Psychology, 84*(3), 261-271.

Aschbacher, P. R. (1993). *Issues in innovative assessment for classroom practice: Barriers and facilitators.* (CSE Technical Report 359). Los Angeles, CA: National Center for Research on Evaluation, Standards and Student Testing.

Asp, E. (1998). The relationship between large-scale and classroom assessment: Compatibility or conflict? In R. Brandt (Ed.), *Assessing student learning: New rules, new realitie*s (17-46). Arlington, VA: Educational Research Service.

Atkin, J. M. (1992). Teaching as research: An essay. *Teaching and Teacher Education, 8*(4), 381-390.

Atkin, J. M. (1994). Teacher research to change policy. In S. Hollingsworth and H. Hockett (Eds.), *Teacher research and educational reform* (103-120), 93rd Yearbook of the National Society for the Study of Education, Part I. Chicago, IL: University of Chicago Press.

Ball, D. L. (1993). With an eye on the mathematical horizon: Dilemmas of teaching elementary school mathematics. *The Elementary School Journal, 93*(4), 373-397.

Bangert-Drowns, R. L., Kulik, C-L. C., Kulik, J. A., & Morgan, M. T. (1991). The instructional effect of feedback in test-like events. *Review of Educational Research, 61*(2), 213 - 238.

Barber, J., Bergman, L., Goodman, J. M., Hosoume, K., Lipner, L., Sneider, C., & Tucker, L. (1995). *Insights and outcomes: Assessments for great explorations in math and science.* Berkeley: University of California, Lawrence Hall of Science.

Baron, J. B. (1991). Strategies for the development of effective performance exercises. *Applied Measurement in Education, 4*(4), 305-318.

Baxter, G. P., Elder, A. D., & Glaser, R. (1996). Knowledge-based cognition and performance assessment in the science classroom. *Educational Psychologist, 31,* 133-140.

Baxter, G. P., & Glaser, R. (1998, Fall). Investigating the cognitive complexity of science assessments. *Educational Measurements: Issues and Practices.*

Baxter, G. P., & Shavelson, R. J. (1994). Science performance assessments: Benchmarks and surrogates. *International Journal of Educational Research, 21,* 279-

298.

Bernauer, J. A., & Cress, K. (1997). How school communities can help redefine accountability assessment. *Phi Delta Kappan, 79*(1), 71-75.

Black, P. J. (1993). Formative and summative assessment by teachers. *Studies in Science Education, 21,* 49-97.

Black, P. J. (1997). *Testing: Friend or foe ? Theory and practice of assessment and testing.* London, England: Falmer Press.

Black, P., & Atkin, M. J. (1996). *Changing the subject: Innovations in science, mathematics and technology education.* London, England: Routledge.

Black, P., & Wiliam, D. (1998a). Assessment and classroom learning. *Assessment in Education, 5*(1), 7-74.

Black, P. & Wiliam, D. (1998b) Inside the black box: Raising standards through classroom assessment. *Phi Delta Kappan, 80*(2), 139-148.

Bol, L., & Strange, A. (1996). The contradiction between teachers' instructional goals and their assessment practices in high school biology courses. *Science Education, 80*(2), 145-163.

Bracey, G. W. (1998). *Put to the test: An educator's and consumer's guide to standardized testing.* Bloomington, IN: Phi Delta Kappa International.

Brown, A. L. (1994). The advancement of learning. *Educational Researcher, 23*(8), 4-12.

Burger, D. (1998). *Designing a sustainable standards-based assessment system: What's noteworthy.* Aurora, CO: Mid-continent Regional Educational Laboratory.

Butler, J. (1995). Teachers judging standards in senior science subjects: Fifteen years of the Queensland experiment. *Studies in Science Education, 26,* 135-157.

Butler, R. (1987). Task-involving and ego-involving properties of evaluation: Effects of different feedback conditions on motivational perceptions, interest and performance. *Journal of Educational Psychology, 79*(4), 474-482.

Butler, R. (1988). Enhancing and undermining intrinsic motivation: The effects of task-involving and ego-involving evaluation on interest and performance. *British Journal of Educational Psychology, 58,* 1-14.

Butler, R., & Neuman, O. (1995). Effects of task and ego-achievement goals on help-seeking behaviours and attitudes. *Journal of Educational Psychology, 87*(2), 261-271.

Cameron, J., & Pierce, D. P. (1994). Reinforcement, reward, and intrinsic motivation: A meta-analysis. *Review of Educational Research, 64*(3), 363-423.

Cangelosi, J. S. (1990). *Designing tests for evaluating student achievement.* New York: Longman.

Cochran-Smith, M., & Lytle, S. (1999). Teacher learning in communities. In A. Iran-Nejad and C. D. Pearson (Eds.), *Review of research in education* (249-306). Washington, DC: American Educational Research Association.

Coffey, J. (2001). Making connections: Student participation in assessment. Unpublished doctoral dissertation, Stanford University, CA.

Cole, K., Coffey, J., & Goldman, S. V. (1999). Using assessments to improve equity in mathematics. *Educational Leadership, 56*(6), 56-58.

Cooper, B., & Dunne, M. (2000). Constructing the real goal of a 'realistic' math item: A comparison of 10-11 and 13-14 year olds. In A. Filer (Ed.), *Assessment: Social practice and social product* (87-109). London, England: RoutledgeFalmer.

Covington, M. L. (1992*). Making the grade: A self-worth perspective on motivation and school reform.* Cambridge, UK: Cambridge University Press.

Crooks, T. J. (1988). The impact of classroom evaluation practices on students. *Review of Educational Research, 58*(4), 438-481.

Cunningham, G. K. (1997). *Assessment in the classroom.* London, England: Falmer Press.

Darling-Hammond, L. (1994). Performance-based assessment and educational equity. *Harvard Educational Review, 64*(1), 5-30.

Darling-Hammond, L., Ancess, J., & Falk, B. (1995). *Authentic assessment in action: Studies of schools and students at work.* New York: Teachers College Press.

Delaware Science Coalition. (1999). *Delaware Comprehensive Assessment Program.* Dover, DE: Author.

Doran, R., Chan, F., & Tamir, P. (1998). *Science educators guide to assessment.*

Arlington, VA: National Science Teachers Association.

Duschl, R.D., & Gitomer, D.H. (1997). Strategies and challenges to changing the focus of assessment and instruction in science classrooms. *Educational Assessment, 4*(1), 37-73.

Dweck, C. S. (1986). Motivational processes affecting learning. *Psychological Science and Education [Special Issue]. American Psychologist, 41*(10), 1040-1048.

Elliot, J. (1987). Educational theory, practical philosophy, and action research. *British Journal of Educational Studies, XXXV*(2), 149-169.

Frederiksen, J. R., & Collins, A. (1989). A systems approach to educational testing. *Educational Researcher, 18*(9) 27-32.

Frederiksen, N. (1984). The real test bias: Influences of testing on teaching and learning. *American Psychologist, 39*, 193-202.

Fuchs, L. S., & Fuchs, D. (1986). Effects of systematic formative evalustion: A meta-analysis. *Exceptional Children, 53*(3), 199-208.

Gallagher, J. D. (1998). Classroom assessment for teachers. Upper Saddle River, NJ: Merrill.

Gifford, B.R., & O'Connor, M.C. (Eds.). (1992). *Changing assessments: Alternative views of aptitude, achievement and instruction.* Boston: Kluwer.

Gipps, C.V. (1994). *Beyond testing: Towards a theory of educational assessment.* London, England: Falmer Press.

Goldman, S.V. (1996). *Unfinished business: How assessment work is managed in school.* Paper presented at the 1996 annual American Anthropology Association meeting, Philadelphia, PA.

Goodlad, J.I. (1984). *A place called school: Promise for the future.* New York: McGraw-Hill.

Gronlund, N. E. (1998). *Assessment of student achievement (6th edition).* Boston: Allyn and Bacon.

Hacker, D. J., Dunlosky, J., & Graesser, A.C. (Eds.). (1998). *Metacognition in educational theory and practice.* Mahwah, NJ: Lawrence Erlbaum.

Hambleton, R. K., Jaeger, R. M., Koretz, D., Linn, R. L., Millman, J., & Phillips, S.E.

(1995). *Review of the measurement quality of the Kentucky Instructional Results Information System,* 1991-1994. Frankfort: Kentucky General Assembly.

Haney, W., & Madaus, G. (1994). *Effects of standardized testing and the future of the national assessment of educational progress.* Chestnut Hill, MA: Center for the Study of Testing, Evaluation and Educational Policy.

Hardy, R. A. (1995). Examining the costs of performance assessment. *Applied Measurement in Education, 8*(2), 121-134.

Hargreaves, A. (1998). *International handbook of educational change.* Dordrecht: Kluwer.

Hein, G., & Price, S. (1994). *Active assessment for active science.* Portsmouth, NH: Heinemann.

Herman, J. L., Gearhart, M., & Baker, E. L. (1993). Assessing writing portfolios: Issues in the validity and meaning of scores. *Educational Assessment, 1*(3), 201-224.

Kluger, A. N., & deNisi, A. (1996). The effects of feedback interventions on performance: A historical review, a meta-analysis, and a preliminary feedback intervention theory. *Psychological Bulletin, 119*(2), 254-284.

Koretz, D., Stecher, B., Klein, S., McCaffrey, D., & Deibert, T. (1993). *Can portfolios assess student performance and influence instruction? The 1991-92 Vermont experience.* (CSE Technical Report Number 371). Los Angeles: National Center for Research on Evaluation, Standards, and Student Testing.

Koretz, D., Stecher, B., Klein, S., & McCaffrey, D. (1994). The Vermont portfolio assessment program: Findings and implications. *Educational Measurement: Issues and Practices, 13*(3), 5-16.

Linn, R. (2000). Assessments and accountability. *Educational Researcher, 29*(2), 4-14.

Linn, R. L., & Burton, E. (1994). Performance-based assessment: Implications of task specificity. *Educational Measurement: Issues and Practice, 13*(1), 5-8, 15.

Loucks-Horsley, S., Hewson, P.W., Love, N., & Stiles, K.E. (1998). *Designing professional development for teachers of science and mathematics.* Thousand Oaks, CA: Corwin Press.

Love, N. (1999 Spring). *Hands-on! 22*(1).

Loyd, B. H., & Loyd, D. E. (1997). Kindergarten through grade 12 standards: A philosophy of grading. In G. D. Phye (Ed.), *Handbook of classroom assessment: Learning, adjustment, and achievement* (481-490). San Diego, CA: Academic Press.

McTighe, J., & Ferrara, S. (1998). *Assessing learning in the classroom*. Washington, DC: National Education Association.

Messick, S. (1989). Validity. In R.L. Linn (Ed.), *Educational measurement (3rd edition)* (13-103). New York: Macmillan.

Messick, S. (1994). The interplay of evidence and consequences in the validation of performance assessments. *Educational Researcher, 23*(2), 13-23.

Mills, R. P., (1996). State portfolio assessment: The Vermont experience. In J. Baron and D. Wolf (Eds.), *Performance-based student assessment: Challenges and possibilities* (192-214). Chicago, IL: National Society for the Study of Education.

Minstrell, J. (1992). Teaching science for understanding. In M. Pearsal (Ed.), *Scope, sequence and coordination of secondary school science: Relevant research volume 2* (237-251). Arlington, VA: National Science Teachers Association.

Moss, P. A. (1994). Can there be validity without reliability? *Educational Researcher, 23*(2), 5-12.

Moss, P. A. (1996) Enlarging the dialogue in educational measurement: Voices from interpretive research traditions. *Educational Researcher, 25*(1), 20-28, 43.

National Research Council. (1981). *Ability testing: Uses, consequences and controversies*. A.K. Wigdor & W.R. Garner (Eds.), Committee on Ability Testing, Commission on Behavioral and Social Sciences and Education. Washington, DC: National Academy Press.

National Research Council. (1987). *Education and learning to think*. L. R. Resnick (Ed.), Committee on Mathematics, Science, and Technology Education, Commission on Behavioral and Social Sciences and Education. Washington, DC: National Academy Press.

National Research Council. (1996). *National science education standards*. National Committee on Science Education Standards and Assessment. Washington, DC: National Academy Press.

National Research Council. (1999a). *How people learn: Brain, experience and school.* J.R. Bransford, A.L. Brown, & R.R. Cocking (Eds.), Committee on Developments in the Science of Learning, Commission on Behavioral and Social Sciences and Education. Washington, DC: National Academy Press.

National Research Council. (1999b). *Testing, teaching, and learning: A guide for states and school districts.* R. Elmore & R. Rothman (Eds.), Committee on Title I Testing and Assessment, Commission on Behavioral and Social Sciences Education. Washington DC: National Academy Press.

National Research Council. (2000). *Inquiry and the national science education standards: A guide for teaching and learning.* S. Olson & S. Loucks-Horsley (Eds.), Committee on the Development of an Addendum to the *National Science Education Standards* on Scientific Inquiry. Washington, DC: National Academy Press.

Oakes, J. (1985). *Keeping track: How schools structure inequality.* New Haven, CT: Yale University Press.

Oakes, J. (1990). *Multiplying inequalities: The effects of race, social class, and tracking on opportunities to learn mathematics and science.* Santa Monica, CA: RAND.

Popham, W. J. (1992). A tale of two-test specification strategies. *Educational Measurement: Issues and Practice, 11*(2), 16-17, 22.

Quellmalz, E. S. (1991). Developing criteria for performance assessments: The missing link. *Applied Measurement in Education, 4*(4), 319-332.

Resnick, L.B, & Resnick, D.P. (1991). Assessing the thinking curriculum: New tools for educational reform. In B. Gifford (Ed.) *Changing assessments: Alternative views of aptitude, achievement and instruction.* Boston, MA: Kluwer.

Roberts, L., Wilson, M., & Draney, K. (1997, June). *The SEPUP assessment system: An overview.* (BEAR Report Series, SA-97-1). Berkeley: University of California Press.

Rosenbaum., J. E. (1980). Social implications of educational grouping. In D.C. Berliner (Ed.) *Review of research in education* (361-

401). Washington, DC: American Educational Research Association.

Rosenthal, R., & Jacobsen, L. (1968). *Pygmalion in the classroom: Teacher expectation and pupils' intellectual development.* New York: Holt, Rinehart and Winston.

Rothman, R. (1995). *Measuring up: Standards, assessment and school reform.* San Francisco: Jossey-Bass.

Rowe, M. B. (1974). Wait time and rewards as instructional variables, their influence on language, logic and fate control: Part one–Wait time. *Journal of Research in Science Teaching, 11,* 87-94.

Rudd, T. J., & Gunstone, R.F. (1993). *Developing self-assessment skills in grade 3 science and technology: The importance of longitudinal studies of learning.* Paper presented at the Annual National Association for Research in Science Teaching, April, Atlanta, GA.

Ruiz-Primo, M. A., & Shavelson, R.J. (1996). Rhetoric and reality in science performance assessments: An update. *Journal of Research in Science Teaching, 33*(10), 1045-1063.

Sadler, R. (1989). Formative assessment and the design of instructional systems. *Instructional Science, 18,* 119-144.

Schunk, D. H., & Zimmerman, B.J. (1998). *Self-regulated learning: From teaching to self-reflective practice.* New York: Guilford Press.

Science Education for Public Understanding Program. (1995). *Issues, evidence and you* (teacher's guide). Ronkonkoma, NY: LabAids.

Seidel, S., Walters, J., Kirby, E., Olff, N., Powell, K., Scripp, L., & Veenema, S. (1997). *Portfolio practices: Thinking through the assessment of student work.* Washington, DC: National Education Association.

Shavelson, R. J., Baxter, G. P., & Pine, J. (1991). Performance assessment in science. *Applied Measurement in Education* [Special Issue: R. Stiggins and B. Plake, Guest Editors], *4*(4), 347-362.

Shavelson, R.J ., & Ruiz-Primo, M. A. (1999). On the assessment of science achievement. *Unterrichts Wissenschaft, 2*(27), 102-127.

Shepard, L. A. (1995). Using assessment to improve learning. *Educational Leadership,* February, 38-43.

Skaalvik, E. M. (1990). Attribution of perceived academic results and relations with self-esteem in senior high school students. *Scandinavian Journal of Educational Research, 34,* 259-269.

Smith, M. L., & Rottenberg, C. (1991). Unintended consequences of external testing in elementary schools. *Educational Measurement: Issues and Practice, 10*(4), 7-11.

Smith, P. S., Hounshell, P. B., Copolo, C., & Wilkerson, S. (1992). The impact of end-of-course testing in chemistry on curriculum and instruction. *Science Education, 76*(5), 523-530.

Stecher, B. M., & Herman, J. L. (1997). Using portfolios for large-scale assessment. In G. D. Phye, (Ed.), *Handbook of classroom assessment* (491-517). San Diego, CA: Academic Press.

Stiggins, R. J. (1999). Learning teams for assessment literacy. (Reprinted from the *Journal of Staff Development, 20*(3),17-21.)

Stiggins, R. J. (2001) *Student-involved classroom assessment (3rd edition).* Columbus, OH: Merrill Prentice Hall.

Tobin, K., & Garnett, P. (1988). Exemplary practice in science classrooms. *Science Education, 72*(2), 197-208

Vispoel, W. P., & Austin, J. R. (1995). Success and failure in junior high school: A critical incident approach to understanding students' attributional beliefs. *American Educational Research Journal, 32*(2), 377-412.

Vygotsky, L. S. (1962). *Thought and language.* New York: Wiley.

Wenger, E. (1998). *Communites of practice: Learning, meaning and identity.* Cambridge, MA: Cambridge University Press.

White, B.Y., & Frederiksen, J. R. (1998). Inquiry, modeling and meta-cognition: Making science accessible to all students. *Cognition and Instruction, 16*(1), 3-118.

Wiggins, G. (1998). *Educative assessment.* San Francisco: Jossey-Bass.

Wiliam, D. (1996). National curriculum assessments and programmes of study: Validity and impact. *British Educational Research Journal, 22*(1), 129-141.

Wiliam, D., & Black, P. J. (1996). Meanings and consequences: A basis for distinguishing formative and summative functions of assessment? *British Educational Research Journal, 22*(5), 537-548.

Wilson, M., & Sloane, K. (1999). *From principles to practice: An embedded assessment system.* (BEAR Report Series, SA-99-3). Berkeley: University of California Press.

Wilson, M., & Draney, K. (1997, July). *Developing maps for student progress in the SEPUP assessment system.* (BEAR Report Series, SA-97-2.) Berkeley: University of California Press.

Wolf, D., Bixby, J., Glen, J. III, & Gardner, H. (1991). *To use their minds well: Investigating new forms of student assessment.* In G. Grant (Ed.), *Review of research in education* (31-74). Washington, DC: American Educational Research Association.

Wood, D., Bruner, J. S., & Ross, G. (1976). The role of tutoring in problem solving, *Journal of Child Psychology and Psychiatry and Allied Disciplines, 17*, 89-100.

Wood, R.(1991) *Assessment and testing: A survey of research.* Cambridge, MA: Cambridge University Press.

# Index

## C

Class discussions, 19, 23-24
Class size, 101-102
Classroom assessment, 7-58
    case for strengthening, 11-21
    equity principle in, 52-55
    formative, 13-15, 25-26, 30-32
    goals for, 32-33, 49-52
    and high standards, 19-20
    key points, 21, 58
    multiple purposes of, 20-21
    present situation, 33-49
    school's role in, 18-19
    student's role in, 17-18
    teacher's role in, 15-17
    validity and reliability of, 55-58
    vignettes of, 5, 26-30, 43-47, 89-95
Collaboration, in professional development, 81-82
Committee on Science Education (COSE K-12), 3
Communicating achievement, 64-65, 68-69
Community involvement, and parents, 103
Conceptions of learning, 87-88
Conversations for assessment, 19
    in vignettes of classrooms, 27
Criteria-setting, 1, 9, 32-33
Criterion-referenced tests (CRTs), 72
Cumulative assessment. *See* Summative assessment
Current reform
    in Connecticut, 76-77
    in Delaware, 89-95
    in Douglas, Colorado, 77
    in Kentucky, 75
    learning from, 74-76
    in Queensland, Australia, 76
    in Vermont, 75

## D

Data. *See* Assessment data
Design of assessment, 16-17, 37
"Disclosure" issues, 54
District level, 99-102
    administrative support, 102
    class size, 101-102
    professional development, 100
    testing policies, 2, 98-99
    time, 100-101

## E

Embedded assessment, 31
Equity principle, 52-55
Esteem. *See* Self-esteem
Evidence and Tradeoffs (ET) Variable, in SEPUP, 68
Experiments, assessment of scientific, 40-47
External assessment
    for consistency, 2
    large-scale, 2, 69, 71-73
    standards-based summative, 73-74

## F

Feedback
    cognitive and affective, 15-16
    giving to students, 86-87
Formative assessment, 4, 25-26, 30-32
    defined, 12, 20, 25
    framework for, 13-15
    grading and communicating achievement, 64-65, 68-69
    relationship to summative, 59-77
    in scientific experimentation, 40-47
Forms
    to match purpose, 35-38
    performance assessments, 60-61
    portfolios, 61-62
    summative assessment in the classroom, 60-64
    traditional tests, 62-64
Framework for formative assessment, 13-15
    and science content, 14-15

## G

Goal achievement, 1, 49-52
    assessment consistent with pedagogy, 51
    assessment data management, 52
    use of assessment data, 51-52, 56
Goals
    establishing, 83-84
    learning, 39
Grading
    of achievement, 64-65, 68-69
    to convey information, 16

## T

Teacher involvement, 15-17, 75-76
  in developing and interpreting standards, 17
  in implementing standards, 15
  role in design, selection and participation, 16-17, 37
  role in external science assessments, 99
  role in feedback, cognitive and affective, 15-16
  using assessment to inform teaching, 1, 9, 12-13, 24
Teachers
  higher education for, 102-103
  performance criteria for, 87
  playing multiple roles, 55
Teaching standards, 50
  developing and interpreting, 17
  implementing, 15
Testing
  criterion-referenced, 72
  district and state policies, 2, 98-99
  norm-referenced, 72
  traditional, 19, 62-64
Testing policies, impacts of, 97-98

Third International Mathematics and Science Study (TIMSS), 2
Time for professional development, providing, 100-101
Timing of assessment, 40
Traditional tests and quizzes, 19
  using differently, 62-64

## U

Understanding
  defining, 36, 85
  identifying, 84-86

## V

Validity concerns, 55-58
  applying to classroom teaching, 71
  in classroom terms, 57-58
  in summative assessments, 69-71
Variety in assessment, 30, 34-35
Vignettes of classrooms, 5, 26-30, 43-47, 89-95

# NATIONAL SCIENCE EDUCATION STANDARDS: A SERIES

## ORDER FORM

| Qty. | Code | Title | Price | Total |
|------|------|-------|-------|-------|
| _____ | CLASS | Classroom Assessment and the national Science Education Standards: A Guide for Teaching and Learning | $18.95 | _____ |
| _____ | DESMAT | Designing Mathematics or Science Curriculum Programs: A Guide for Using Mathematics and Science Education Standards | $12.95 | _____ |
| _____ | TEAPRE | Improving Teacher Preparation and Credentialing Consistent with the National Science Education Standards | $15.00 | _____ |
| _____ | INQSCT | Inquiry and the National Science Education Standards: A Guide for Teaching and Learning | $21.95 | _____ |
| _____ | INTRO | Introducing the National Science Education Standards, Booklet | $ 1.95 | _____ |
| _____ | SCISTT | National Science Education Standards | $19.95 | _____ |
| _____ | INSMAT | Selecting Instructional Material: A Guide for K-12 Science | $18.95 | _____ |
| | | | Subtotal | _____ |
| | | | Shipping | _____ |
| | | | Tax | _____ |
| | | | **TOTAL** | _____ |

Use this form to order additional copies of **Classroom Assessment and the National Science Education Standards** and other books from the series. All orders must be prepaid. Please add $4.50 for shipping and handling for the first copy ordered and $0.95 for each additional copy. If you live in CA, DC, FL, MD, MO, TX, or Canada, add applicable sales tax or GST. Prices apply only in the United States, Canada, and Mexico and are subject to change without notice.

___ I am enclosing a check/money order payable to

   National Academy Press for $_____.

___ I am enclosing a purchase order.

___ Please charge my VISA/MasterCard/American Express account.

Number: _____ Expiration: _____

Signature:_____

*Please print.*

Name: _____

Address:_____

City: _____ State: _____ ZIP: _____

Phone:_____ E-mail: _____

6998

---

### 📖 FOUR EASY WAYS TO ORDER 📖

**By phone:** Call toll-free (888) 624-8422 or (202) 334-3313
**By fax:** Fax your order to (202) 334-2451
**By Internet:** Order via our Website at www.nap.edu
**By mail:** Send your order with payment to
   **National Academy Press**
   2101 Constitution Avenue, NW
   Lockbox 285
   Washington, DC 20055

*Customers in North America Only. All international customers please contact National Academy Press for export prices and ordering information.*